W9-BBY-447

WHAT PEOPLE ARE SAYING ABOUT CARLA...

When Carla first shared that she intended to write her story, I rejoiced for the many people I know will be transformed by her story of resilience, self-realization, and empowerment. Carla has a gift; few people can tell their story the way Carla does. With humor, empathy, and a genuine desire to help people reach their true potential, Carla has made it her life's work to share that hope with others. I've had the pleasure of knowing Carla as a colleague and friend. Her hunger to live life to the fullest is infectious and permeates her personal and professional relationships. She finds every opportunity to encourage and exhort those around her to live with purpose and to always bring their best professionally and personally. She is a brand ambassador for living life with conviction, humility, and a genuine joy. Carla is the true definition of the servant leader; someone who puts others first and isn't afraid to take their hand and walk with them to show them the way. In her signature style, *Crash!* is written in a relatable and understandable manner, but get ready to do some work! Ms. Carla Moore will challenge you to unpack what's holding you back and make a true commitment to break through!

Bernadette Aulestia
EVP, Global Distribution
HBO

Leadership: science or art form? I suppose compelling arguments might be made to support either. And there certainly are powerful individuals to whom one might assign either characterization. And then there are the Carla Moores of this world, who seem to embody some quality of leadership for which no one definitional silo seems to be an exact fit. My earliest experiences of Carla occurred when she was involved with the Chicago chapter of the National Association for Multi-ethnicity in Communications, for which I have headed up education and diversity initiatives for over a decade. I recall having thought, "Who is this woman? She's not a panel expert this evening, yet every word out of her mouth seems to reposition their lofty messages with almost breathtaking clarity." As our relationship as colleagues and friends has matured, I've never ceased to be impressed with her ability to raise the learning temperature of the room, to shift the conversation from platitudes to passionate, engaged, useful meaning. That she has now captured some of this in her first book hardly comes as an ineluctable next-step for a person of her gifts. I'm just glad I wasn't the person with the unenviable task of editing her words. Must be tantamount to instructing Callas how interpret Puccini.

James C. Jones

Senior Vice President, Education and Diversity Solutions

NAMIC, Inc.

What a brilliantly delivered experience! Carla took me on a spiritual journey that was so spellbinding, inspiring, and profound that I felt I had gone to church in the middle of the NAMIC conference! It started when I heard her soulful voice singing Nina Simone's "Feeling Good" from the back of the room and as she made her way up and introduced herself, I knew we were in for a treat. And then she started: "It was a Tuesday ..."

Yasmine Ndassa, PhD

Sr Director, Business Process Analytics

Comcast Cable

Carla Moore is an amazing speaker! Never heard anyone like her before. Moore mesmerized the audience and kept us wanting more. She crafts her personal story like she is sitting with old friends—all the while inspiring everyone in her space. Her standout singing entrance into the room was stunning and lingered even as she told her story. She is not one to miss!

Sandra Rice
SVP, National Recruitment and Leadership Development
Emma Bowen Foundation

Riveting and motivating. Carla's story touches the soul and beautifully awakens our potential. She empowers us to rise and live fearlessly while supporting and celebrating others.

Aunree J. Houston
Vice President, Sales
HBO

Carla has helped develop me into a successful woman, sister, friend, and physician. She has given me constructive feedback in order to thrive as a leader, whether making critical decisions on the hospital floor or setting goals for my next direction in life. She is iron, constantly sharpening others and keeping everyone on point. I know this book can only lead to others' continuous success and fulfillment. Carla's impact allows you to see that the wreckage is an opportunity. I am thankful everyday for the roadmap she helped me build while driving through life.

Dr. Victoria Thomas
University of Chicago
Pritzker School of Medicine Alumna

Carla Moore's NAMIC Ted Talk was noteworthy, inspiring, and thought provoking. Her ability to captivate a room with her wit and life experience was impactful and awesomely refreshing. I was personally affected by her testimony and left with a desire to take a personal inventory of my life. As a result of this self-assessment, I have made some immediate changes to move toward my best life.

Ingrid Hadley
Employee Resource Group Manager
NBCUniversal

Carla Moore is the embodiment of life goals. Her brand is strong and whether I overhear her in the halls at work or on a stage speaking, I feel energized and take away something new that applies to me personally or professionally. Her transparency and inspirational nature evokes a feeling in everyone who meets her!

Carolyn Githieya
Account Executive
HBO

I had been through so much in my life and didn't know how to deal with the trauma I endured as a child. It showed up in all aspects of my life even through adulthood and I didn't know what my purpose for living was. I didn't know how to see my way through the darkness. My husband, Telly, had experienced similar challenges in his life and we struggled to communicate effectively to meet each other's needs. I remember sitting on my living room floor praying to God for guidance to help my family overcome that difficult time in our lives. I received a call from Carla and my prayers had been answered. From that day forward, Carla has helped me heal the little girl inside of me to see my true potential. Carla has helped my husband to identify his strengths and weaknesses and has given him the tools needed to live in the moment and not in the past. He is more confident now than he has ever been. Carla's life coaching has had a tremendous impact on our lives. She has helped us to see that what we have endured in the past does not define our destiny and that we are in control of our lives and we can live the life we imagined. We are so very blessed to have the experience of life coaching sessions with Carla.

Ashley Outlaw
Coaching Client
Student

It is not often I have sat in a room filled with women and felt as if the panelist was speaking words of inspiration directly to me in a private conversation. Being in Carla's presence and hearing her words at the Women in Communications event was beyond empowering. Carla lit a fire within me and empowered me to believe that anything I desired in life was achievable. The day after hearing her speak, I immediately decided I would no longer feel stuck in my former position. I completely rewrote my resume and sought opportunities that would propel me to the next step in my career. I now work at HBO as Carla's colleague by day, and am a law student by night. I am still aspiring for more. I saw Carla speak almost three years ago and I am still as motivated by her words now as I was then.

Alyssa Reid
Business Affairs
HBO

I met Carla while an intern at HBO ... and instantly, I found a mentor, an ally and a voice of reason. Carla's trajectory, both personal and professional, imbue her with the sixth sense of hearing what you don't say and knowing what you're seeking. And I have been the beneficiary of these talents more than once. No matter her schedule, the distance and the time zone, Carla has made time for me whenever I've reached out to her and created a safe space for deep discussion. I am forever grateful to her for her wisdom and infectious laugh.

Nayna Agrawal
Screen and Film Writer

The time I spent working with Carla was the best education in leadership I could have asked for. Front he flawless example she provides of how to truly live to your core values to the way she can expertly deliver the right dose of tough love, Carla is constantly raising the game of her team. Her sense of self emanates from every word and action, yet her keen eye is quick to recognize the unique talents of those around her and cultivate them to their full potential. Carla is the ultimate leader, not to mention a friend and a mentor; she brings out the best in all of us.

Val Kaplan Mike
Sr. Product Manager
Hulu

CRASH!

CRA

LEADING THR

GH THE WRECKAGE

CARLA MOORE

ForbesBooks

Published by ForbesBooks, Charleston, South Carolina.
Member of Advantage Media Group.

Printed in the United States of America.

10 9 8 7 6 5 4 3 2 1

ISBN: 978-1-946633-05-7
LCCN: 2017963496

Cover and layout design by George Stevens.

This publication is designed to provide accurate and authoritative information in regard to the subject matter covered. It is sold with the understanding that the publisher is not engaged in rendering legal, accounting, or other professional services. If legal advice or other expert assistance is required, the services of a competent professional person should be sought.

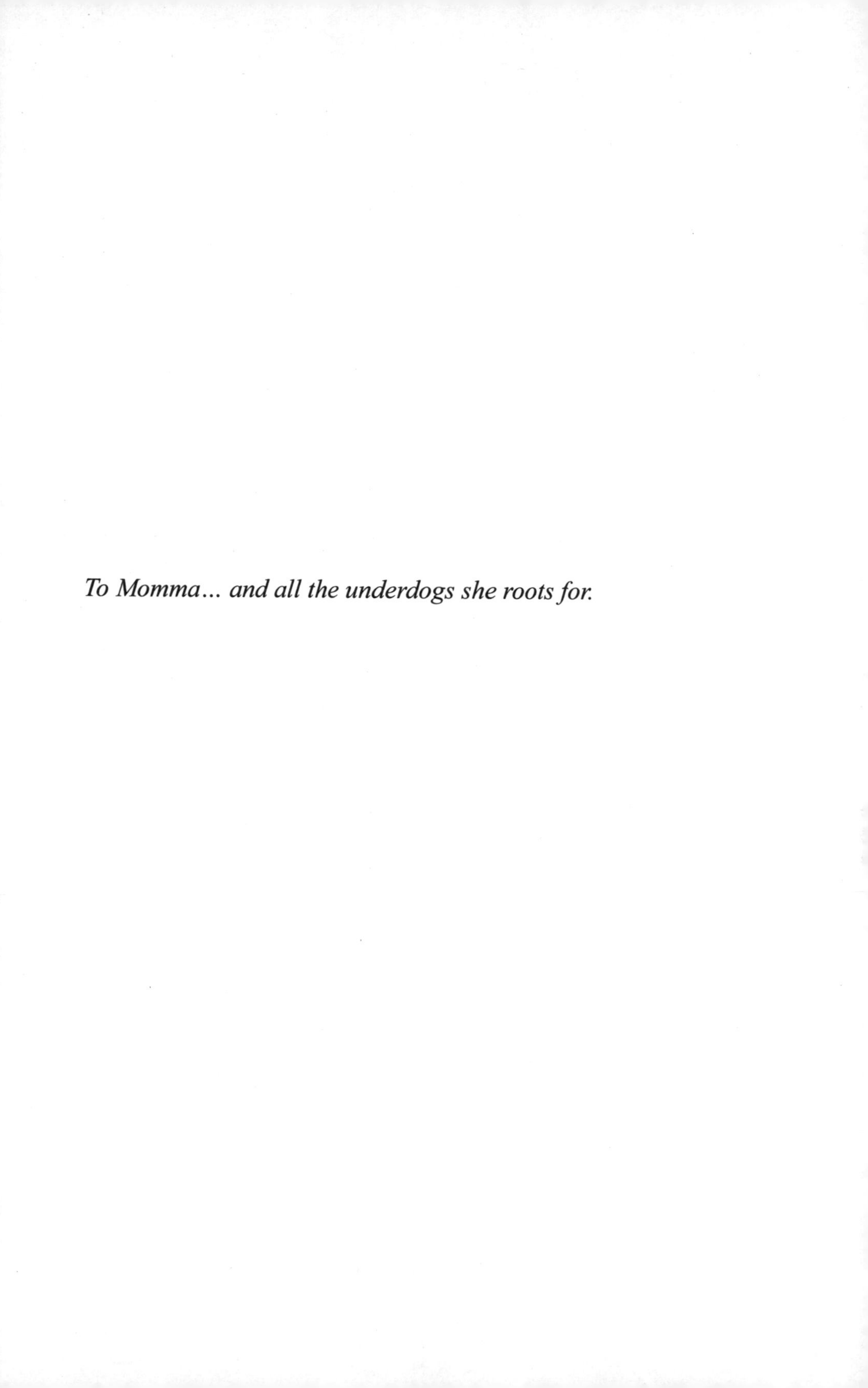

To Momma… and all the underdogs she roots for.

TABLE OF CONTENTS

FOREWORD

Research suggests we will meet close to 80,000 individuals over the course of our lives. Among the multitudes, there are certain standouts who can only be described as phenomenal. Carla's personal and professional story isn't one you encounter casually—her story is an experience.

I first met Carla via her application into a leadership development program I was managing. Before I was able to fully review her application, her sponsor called. Her sponsor shared with me that Carla was bigger than her phenomenal resume. After working with more than 8,700 global executives at the Center for Creative Leadership, the Executive Leadership Council, and The Network of Executive Women, Carla's application is by far the most memorable. The leadership development programs I've hosted over the past fifteen years have been full of C-suite executives. I've seen excellent talent so often I'm no longer impressed by anything less. Yet Carla, even on paper, is far superior to excellent. Her story, inspiring. Her essence, humble. Carla is as experienced as they get, with a journey that spans boots on the ground to stilettos in the boardroom. Her story is nothing short of inspiring. I've shared her story in public settings more than a dozen times ... her story never ceases to inspire and affect audiences large and small.

CRASH! is her story. Designed for you to experience her journey word by carefully chosen word, *CRASH!* provides a unique personal message to enable readers to design their own roadmap to unprecedented success and happiness. *CRASH!* is a feel-good book that awakens and empowers the leader in everyone. The great part of her story is that we share it with her as if it's ours—because her experiences and lessons are universal.

CRASH! is the "How-To" guide to driving into your fulfilled future while preventing you from leaving YOUR experience half lived.

—Robbie Solomon, PhD
Director of Talent Development
Network of Executive Women (NEW)

ACKNOWLEDGMENTS

I've always been a small-town girl with big dreams. The only way I've even made it to where I am today has been on the wings and prayers of those who raised me, cheered for me, and loved me.

I want to humbly acknowledge my Momma, Clara Moore, who sacrificed her own dreams for all of ours. She taught us unconditional love, perseverance, resilience, and how to plug into Higher Power. Everything I am and everything I hope to become I owe to you, Momma, for teaching us about the power of God. I know I am nothing without Him. Thank you, Daddy, for your humor and for showing us how to laugh at almost anything.

I wish to express my deep affection, love, and appreciation for my sisters Mimi, Hobrina, Kindra, and my deceased brother Victor. The illustration of my life is a combination of all of you within me. To my nephews DJ and Trey and only niece Tori, you three are really what makes family magical. (And my brothers in law Doug, Mike, and AT are amazing, too!)

I would like to honor my best friend of over twenty years, Beatrice Hurey, for sharing the walk into womanhood with me and never letting me feel alone. It's funny that, at some point, I became you and you became me.

I also pay homage to the HBO women and men who have made me the leader I am today. Most of my leadership growth and development happened in the walls in HBO Atlanta, HBO Chicago, and HBO New York. Thank you, HBO leaders, for showing me what managerial courage looks like and giving me room to test it out.

I extend profound gratitude to my professional, civic, and social organizations for allowing me to sharpen skills I might not otherwise have had the opportunity to do so early in my career: NAMIC (National Association For Multi-Ethnicity in Communications), WICT (Women in Cable and Telecommunications), NBMBAA (National Black MBA Association), and Delta Sigma Theta Sorority, Inc. (DST). Later, my connections with CFT (Coaching for Transformation certification program at the New York Open Center), ownership of The Growth Coach franchise, NEW (Network of Executive Women), and Hallmark took me to the next level.

To my coaching clients, participants in my workshops, and attendees at speaking events—I wrote this book based on your encouragement to do so. It was your uplifting and supportive words after each session that fueled me and led to me want to expand my reach. The stories you shared one by one, the tears we shared, the connection we felt made me see this book as a humble offering of service to the world. Thank you for seeing something greater in me.

I must extend profound gratitude to Eland Mann—writer, editor, believer. Thank you for taking my rough drafts, rough calls, and bringing them to life. Thank you for caring for this project as if it were your own. Special thanks to my first editor, Hannah Kohl, who's voice might as well have been my own. Thank you to my publishers, Advantage Media Group and ForbesBooks, and also to my digital media agency, Webimax, for believing this project could be meaningful to the world.

I certainly pay tribute to sister-friends, Sorors and good friends who literally and figuratively carried me through rough patches and had my back: Adrienne Robinson, Zenitra Perry Barrett, Victoria Thomas, Robert Solomon, Sharon Frances Moore (no relation) and her creative video production team, Katrina Brown (my personal and life assistant), and the DB Bistro Family (for laughter, good food, and good wine!). To a very special friend, Anthony Nurse, who taught me compromise, patience, and forgiveness, and was instrumental in my personal expansion and development. Special heartfelt thanks to Sharon Brown and Steven Filante, my CFT instructors. Thank you, Sharon, as my personal coach and friend, for keeping me clear on who I am and the vision for my life. I could not have done any of this without each and every one of you and your belief in me.

To the many kind and loving people in all the places I've lived: Centerville, Murfreesboro, Nashville, Kansas City, Atlanta, Minneapolis, Chicago, New York (in that order) thank you for bringing me into your cities, your homes, your worlds.

And, of course, where would I be without those who have freely given their time, hearts, resources, connections, prayers, and blessings. I cherish everyone who has ever touched my life.

ABOUT THE AUTHOR

Carla's new book *CRASH!* captures the lightning moment that led to her epiphany about the role of personal transformation in improving leadership. Carla openly shares the story of her own transformation from 300 pounds to triathlete and how it unexpectedly transformed her leadership, inspired team members, quickly drove business results, and ultimately, fueled her career. Readers will gain easy-to-use tools and be inspired to activate their own personal power and *live the life they've imagined!*

Armed with her small-town roots and big city dreams, Carla's twenty-year career with HBO began as a sales trainer in Atlanta and then she moved to Chicago and became director a few years later. Today Carla is in New York City where she is currently Vice President of Sales Strategy and Education. Her department develops new sales strategies, designs sales training curriculum, and oversees continuous education programs for sales brand ambassadors.

Before transitioning to her current role, Carla was Vice President of Domestic Network Distribution, leading a sales and marketing team that served over four million HBO and Cinemax subscribers. Her team crafted sales strategies to drive subscriber growth through marketing campaigns promoting HBO original series and movies. Carla also credits her two year stint as Vice President of Talent Acquisition at HBO as helping her to refine her career development coaching for colleagues and many others in and outside of the industry.

Carla is also a new author, aspiring blogger, transformation speaker, and certified professional coach, each to help make her role more meaningful and impactful at HBO and the other organizations she's involved with.

Chicago Tribune, Cosmopolitan Magazine, Forbes, BoldTV, and other outlets have featured Carla for her transformation work. She is a frequent speaker, delivering conference keynotes, facilitating workshops and breakout sessions, webinar host, and is a popular panelist at leadership summits and career management events.

LANE 0

CRASH!

Work. Life. Balance. Compartmentalizing. Separation of work and play. Division of your work self and your true self. We speak about these things as if there is some magical barrier we pass through each day as we leave the warm comforts of our homes and prepare ourselves for the business day, as if we can transform ourselves by shifting bodies, shifting mindsets ... as if who we are in one place is completely separate from who we are in another ... as if what happens in one place doesn't affect what happens in another.

I get it. I used to think that way, too.

On Tuesday, September 18, 2007, I found myself in a circumstance that literally broke me wide open. And while it hurt like nothing I've ever experienced before, it also opened my eyes and showed me there was another way to exist, putting me on a new path in life—one I haven't veered from yet, and never will.

The day was sunny and bright when I landed at Chicago's O'Hare Airport, returning from the annual NAMIC conference in New

York. Being in an airport was something I'd done hundreds—perhaps thousands—of times before. Traveling was a part of my work and I'd been on the road at least three days a week for the past ten years. As an entry level sales trainer charged with ensuring that thousands of cable customer service reps across multiple states and the Caribbean had the product knowledge to sell HBO and Cinemax, I was the queen of business trips.

I had my routine down pat. Carry-on luggage. Car parked in my preferred lot. I was on autopilot as I dropped my single piece of luggage in the trunk, jumped into my car, punched in my favorite radio station, and made my way off the service road and onto I-294 South, heading home for some much-needed rest. It was high noon and I had not yet put the top down; the sun beamed through a cloudless sky as the wind blew through my hair and across my face. It felt wonderful.

IT WAS HIGH NOON AND I HAD NOT YET PUT THE TOP DOWN.

As I rolled down the highway, I was thinking about how good the conference had been and looking forward to sharing with my team some new business growth strategies I'd learned. I distinctly remember I was also thinking about how my expense report was two months behind; *I need to have my assistant help me with all these receipts scattered everywhere*, I was saying to myself. My thoughts wandered next to the fact that my senior vice president was visiting in two weeks for our "all-hands" meeting and how I'd yet to prepare the agenda. To top it off, my cleaning lady was supposed to stop by while I was gone. I wondered if she—

BOOM!

Tires screeching, mind wheeling, everything speeding up in a rocking blur as time slowed and stretched out for miles. Then, nothing.

Less than five minutes from the airport, going fifty-five miles an hour, I'd crashed my convertible car head-on into the concrete median—and I hadn't been wearing a seatbelt. Unaware of what had happened, I simply lay there on my side, tossed onto the passenger seat. Vaguely, I waited for the lights of my life to blink out one by one, and for the scenes of my time on earth to scroll through my mind.

Instead, I saw a man standing and banging at my window telling me that he'd called an ambulance and it was on the way. As he spoke, I became aware that my leg was throbbing. My face burned and shattered glass was everywhere. I was still too confused to understand what was going on. *Why was there an ambulance?*

Then it hit me: I'd been in a massive car accident. Terrified I'd hit someone else, my mind scanned through dark places where memories should've been. I must have spoken out loud because the man said, "No, it was just you." *Just me.*

And then those dark places began to populate with what had happened, as my mind and body roared in protest and pain. I'd been so disconnected from the present moment, so distracted by thoughts of expense reports, my boss coming, the cleaning lady—that I hadn't realized all the cars in front of me had stopped. I had been staring forward at the road ahead of me, but not *seeing* anything. By the time I saw the sea of red taillights, I was nearly on top of them. Without any other choice, I slammed on my breaks, then lost control and hit the concrete median. My car bounced off the concrete, did three screeching donuts in the middle of the highway, and ended up on the other side of the shoulder facing forward … remarkably—and thankfully—all without touching another car.

From that moment, things happened quickly. The ambulance arrived, the EMTs loaded me in the ambulance and the next thing I knew, I was on an emergency-room table. The doctor came over to me and said, "Miss Moore, I just read the EMT report, and your car was totaled." *Totaled!* I blinked my eyes as the doctor continued. "I don't know how you are awake, how nothing is broken, or how you're still lucid and talking. Most people don't make it out of a crash like this."

She let that sink in, and suddenly the magnitude of what happened hit me with an impact even stronger than the physical crash I just survived. I looked up at the doctor and said, "Oh, my gosh. If I had died today, I would've died not living the life I'd imagined."

I LOOKED UP AT THE DOCTOR AND SAID, "OH, MY GOSH. IF I HAD DIED TODAY, I WOULD'VE DIED NOT LIVING THE LIFE I'D IMAGINED."

The truth was that my weight had been fluctuating between 250 and 350 pounds; I was single, turning forty, and I still hadn't figured out my life. Despite my outward academic and career success, internally I was miserable. While I'd done so much in Chicago—earned my MBA, joined industry associations, and really started to move my career—the life I *really* wanted had only been a vision in my head for the past twenty years.

The morning after the crash, I was home, sitting alone in my house, my leg in a brace, my knee bandaged, and my face covered with stitches. I looked around. No car in the garage, obviously, and no one by my side to comfort or help me. It was *just me*. I took a shuddering breath and said to myself, *Girl, this is it. There's a reason you made it out of that wreck. Get it together.* I grabbed a sheet of paper and wrote down exactly what I wanted for my life—things I'd wanted for myself for two decades, but never accomplished.

- Lose one hundred pounds.
- Run a 5k.
- Reactivate community service duties.
- See Rome.

I took those dreams out of my head and put them down on paper, where I could see them. Where they became real. Where I could run my fingers across them, tracing the letters in a tangible, tactile way. There they were in black and white, no longer dreams, but a checklist of must-do's.

What happened in the year after the crash is a story most people say is impossible, but it's one I'm still living today. And it's a story I think can help *you* connect to your own potential, passion, and purpose in life—a story I believe will help you reconcile the compartmentalized pieces of your life and give you the courage and confidence to walk forward as a whole person, equally as strong and healthy in your personal life as you are in your professional life—because there is no separation between the two.

Within a year of the accident, I had lost one hundred pounds; ran my first 5k (and subsequent triathlon); reactivated memberships in my church, sorority, and civic organizations; and became committee chairs in each. I had also spent two weeks in Rome on a solo vacation. A twenty-year vision came to life in just one year. I didn't know the power I already possessed to change my very own life.

I DIDN'T KNOW THE POWER I ALREADY POSSESSED TO CHANGE MY VERY OWN LIFE.

My wake-up call came from a literal, physical crash—an impact that affected my body, then extended spiritually and emotionally to my entire being. My goal in this book is to extend what I learned even further—to you, without leaving you stranded on your sofa in bandages, but with no less of a life-long impact.

I want to use what I've learned to help you connect to your own personal power, so you too can live the life you've imagined. So you too can begin carving a path forward to the next level of yourself, to the life you want at home and at work.

The biggest unexpected learning from all this was seeing myself change as a leader at work. I became much more authentically invested in the overall health and growth of the lives and careers of the people around me. Getting clear about who I was and what I was here to do allowed me to stop focusing so much on myself and my own next achievements.

As I gained more clarity and awareness around my passions and purpose, there was no longer a need to compete and prove. Leadership is not about showing how good you are, it's about showing others how good *they* are.

I believe personal enlightenment is essential for meaningful and impactful leadership. I call it *enlightened leadership*. Enlightened leaders seek to build open and healthy team cultures that raise employee engagement and retention, which we all know drives productivity and profitability. When leaders grow, teams grow, and businesses grow.

In the pages of this book, I openly share my road to personal and professional transformation. How I moved through the wreckage of my life—low self-love, low self-esteem, low self-care, morbid obesity, spiritual bankruptcy, personal emptiness, and habitual loneliness—to now living the life I'd imagined.

Each lane (chapter) provides practical, actionable tools to help drive change and shifts in your own life at home and at work.

While reading this book you will notice features like real, everyday language for easy comprehension. What good is sharing your thoughts if people can't understand your point? There are also "fuel for thought" callouts that hopefully make you pause for a moment and let the concepts sink in. You'll also encounter "pit stop" exercises for personal reflection and for you to complete, now or later. Doing these exercises will uncover roadblocks and open pathways to help you design your roadmap to the live you've imagined. The sooner you face and overcome your boundaries, the closer you are to living your dream.

When you finish this book you will:

- See that "crash moments" are transformations in disguise.
- Have the tools to get you through the wreckage and back on your feet.
- Realize it takes a personal transformation to drive a leadership transformation.

Walking in your dreams is an amazing feeling, and I want everyone to experience it. If you feel like you've stalled out on your way to your dream life, then *Crash!* is the spark for your jumpstart!

LANE 1

"THE TWO MOST IMPORTANT DAYS IN YOUR LIFE: THE DAY YOU WERE BORN AND THE DAY YOU FIND OUT WHY."

—MARK TWAIN

KNOW YOUR MAKE AND MODEL

The first lesson I learned after my car crash was this: You've got to know your make and model. In other words, to really live, you *must know yourself.* I didn't know this back when I was walking across the stage to get my MBA. I didn't know this when I was on cruise-control at work, moving through airports, living life in a daze. I didn't know this when my car hit a median at fifty-five miles per hour and ejected me into the air. I didn't know this when I was laid out on 294 South. I didn't have a clue about who I truly was and what I was truly after.

Lane 1 is the most important chapter in this book and in life. Self-knowledge is the foundation to any type of transformation. You need to know what you're made of, how fast you can go, and what kind of storms you can weather. Knowing who you are, down to the very core, is fundamental to leadership. You must have clarity about what makes you come alive, what drives your creativity, what your non-negotiables are, and where your power comes from. It's this ability to look yourself in the eye and tell the truth that allows you to connect to the very foundation your world is built upon—whether at home, at work, at school, at church, at play, relationship-wise, or anything else. And as with anything else, the best place to start is at the beginning.

LANE 1 IS THE MOST IMPORTANT CHAPTER IN THIS BOOK AND IN LIFE. SELF-KNOWLEDGE IS THE FOUNDATION TO ANY TYPE OF TRANSFORMATION.

DEFINING MOMENTS

Centerville, Tennessee. Population: three thousand (if you're being generous.) That's where I started out.

Even at five, I knew I was different, and I was pretty sure the other kids sensed it, too. Not only was I the heaviest child in my kindergarten, I was one of only two or three other black children in my classroom. At home I was the heaviest and darkest-skinned in my family. Still, I knew my parents loved me and during those first moments on my own in the world, I sat with quiet excitement, proud to show my good manners, eager to show that I cared about school, and taking in my new surroundings as the other children filled the room.

School was a place that held special significance for my parents. Despite being in the minority of our town in terms of skin color, Momma and Daddy were also two of the few college-educated adults in our community. From what my parents told me, I knew that school was a magical place. School was the key to growing up with a rich mind filled with the knowledge I'd need to become a good citizen and make my contribution to the world.

But no one told me there were other things to learn at school aside from book lessons.

The boy at the center of the trouble was small for his age and frail. Even before class started, a group of boys had been picking on him—poking him, teasing him, showing him he wasn't wanted. The bullying continued as the teacher read us a story, then spilled out onto the playground at recess where it quickly escalated into punching and then pushing the boy over, pushing him down.

I saw the boy shaking in fear, utterly alone and in danger, and I had the strangest feeling. Just one day before, we'd all been babies, at home with our mothers, and now, here we were—kindergartners, out in the world where big boys pushed down small boys and made them afraid. How could this happen at *school*—our magical, important, and sacred school?

"Stop!" I heard a loud voice call out. "Leave him alone!" Someone approached the bullies with determined strides and they scattered. The boy looked up, and I saw my own hand reaching down to help him up. The big voice I'd heard yelling "stop" had come from my own mouth. The legs that had taken such determined strides toward the center of the trouble were my own.

The action I took that day taught me an important lesson. Though I didn't have the words for it then, I found I had an innate sense of justice—of right and wrong—and I was willing to put myself on the line and live those beliefs, even at risk to my own safety and popularity.

I have a saying now: "I sacrifice popularity for effectiveness." It was true that day on the playground in Centerville, Tennessee, and it's true today as I lead my team members at HBO to find their own success. "Selfless commitment to justice in action" is a component that shapes who I am, how I think, why I act, and the way I make split-second decisions—but in the years between kindergarten and slamming my car into that concrete median, I'd somehow lost sight of that. I'd lost sight of a lot of other things, as well. Ultimately, it took a literal car crash to lead me of out that mental, and now physical, wreckage and to bring true focus to my leadership and my life. Currently as VP of Point of Sale Strategy and Education at HBO, it's my assignment to not only help develop new sales approach strategies and continuous education programs for our sales brand ambassadors, but also to help people connect to that part of themselves that knows joy, self-worth, self-care, passion, and purpose.

IN THE YEARS BETWEEN KINDERGARTEN AND SLAMMING MY CAR INTO THAT CONCRETE MEDIAN, I'D SOMEHOW LOST SIGHT OF THAT. I'D LOST SIGHT OF A LOT OF OTHER THINGS, AS WELL. ULTIMATELY, IT TOOK A LITERAL CAR CRASH TO LEAD ME OF OUT THAT MENTAL, AND NOW PHYSICAL, WRECKAGE AND TO BRING TRUE FOCUS TO MY LEADERSHIP AND MY LIFE.

PIT STOP!

Personal Ramp: Recall one of your defining moments—a time when your true colors came through. What can you use from that moment to show up in the world today?

____

____

____

____

____

Professional Ramp: Take a look back at this past week at work. Did you experience a defining moment that demonstrated your true self? If yes, write how you can achieve something like that next week. If no, write down what you can do next week to show others who you are.

____

____

____

____

____

THE GRAND CHARADE

> **"The value you're born with will always be greater than anything you can add to it."**
>
> ***–Carla Moore***

After my crash, as I began to transform personally, I noticed a direct correlation with what was happening in my personal life and what was taking place in my leadership at work. I saw it happen immediately, but at first, I didn't acknowledge it for what it was. You see, I had been living a "grand charade" most of my life. I pretended to be happier than I really was. I brushed off heartbreak as if it didn't matter. As long as I had my college degrees, a good job, and money to burn on clothes, bags, shoes, and jeans (I had over forty pairs ... but that's another story.), I told myself I was just fine—thriving. Truthfully, though, I was barely hanging on physically, emotionally, and spiritually. By day, I appeared happy and successful by the world's standards—but each night, I was failing miserably, overwhelmed by sadness, darkness, and consuming large volumes of food.

Then, as I began to grow and expand my self-awareness at home, in my social scenarios, in my physical appearance—and in all of the other roles I was playing in life—I stopped *pretending* to be and just started *being*. Whatever I was feeling or thinking inside, I brought out into the open, sharing with others my thoughts and observations about who I was and what I was going through. I began to openly expose the hurt and pain and insecurities I had been feeling. When I did, I learned other people shared the same struggles, as well as others all their own. I was becoming truthful and honest with myself and with the people I loved.

In the words of famous author and poet Oscar Wilde: "Be yourself. Everyone else is already taken."

FUEL FOR THOUGHT

Sure, there's an incredible amount of vulnerability and risk in living a wholly truthful life, but after the crash, it became the most comfortable way for me to live. The thought of being so vulnerable makes people shy away from doing this, but I learned that no other way of living really works. When you hide your true self, too much energy is spent on living two lives. All that energy could be better spent if it were concentrated on simply living the best life possible.

Once I achieved more clarity, I dropped all the pretenses and started saying to the world, "This is who I am, and this is who I want to become."

I always had an intense personality and a strong drive for achievement and success, but paradoxically, my ambition also kept me feeling inadequate, always needing to compete and prove my worth. Now, I wanted to become the woman who knew she was already good enough regardless of titles, degrees, or dress size. I knew I still harbored some anger and jealousy, but I wanted to learn and live true forgiveness. While I celebrated my single life, I now wanted to share my life and be part of a healthy, fulfilling relationship with someone who respected and loved me unconditionally. So, for the first time, I said these things about myself for all to hear.

I started sharing my true self (more about "True Self" in Lane 10). I started out sharing things about myself to my best friend—things I'd not even told her. From stalled-out dreams and frustrations to my ideal lifestyle, she did not flicker. She was not judgmental and just let me be. In fact, she allowed me to be vulnerable to the point of emotional pain—and I still felt safe with her. That is the true definition of an anchor relationship. This circle only expanded to a few more people early on. After a while, it felt so good to say out loud what I've kept inside. I started sharing everything with anyone who'd listen. It was like I wanted to tell my story before anyone else tried to.

Instead of losing people's respect or interest, I found that they actually continued to love and embrace me. I didn't have to put on any airs. I didn't have to pretend. I didn't have to beg for approval. I could also stop expending so much energy trying to be worthy of people's love and respect, which was absolutely exhausting. I felt a sense of release and relief as I let go of this exhausting, meaningless, mindless behavior. It hadn't served me well, and now I was done with it. In its place, I found myself breathing more deeply and sleeping more soundly as energy flowed back into me.

The strangest thing was that as I became honest with myself about who I was and what was important to me, I saw people respond to me with what could only be described as a sense of relief. I wasn't pretending anymore, and suddenly, they didn't have to pretend with me either. Instead of begging for their complicity, I released them from the grand charade to interact with me on an authentic level. That energized the people around me, first in my personal life and social circles, and then at work, too. I realized when I was truthful about all these aspects of my life, the people around me connected to my honesty. My willingness to be who I really was—and then to stand on it, move on it, and let it be the fuel to drive me—made a difference in my relationships. I was being the me I was meant to be—and people still wanted to be around me, still wanted to be friends, still wanted to be connected to me.

Today, a little more than a decade after the crash that didn't take my life but saved it, I am maintaining nearly a one hundred fifty-pound weight loss, still enjoying a growing career, touching lives, and helping others; it all comes down to being crystal clear about who I am, what I want, what I'm here to do, and what I'm in it for. I can take care of my body because I thoroughly know and love myself; I have clarity and awareness around who I am, what I'm meant to be, and what I need to do to get there. Today, I wholeheartedly understand my worth, and the decisions I make are aligned with that understanding. Choices shape destiny and I no longer choose harm for myself.

As I started to understand that concept on a personal level, I brought it to work with me. The depth of my own transformation that touched every area of my life sealed my destiny, my purpose. I believe the purpose of my life is to engage and inspire others to carve a path forward to live the life they've imagined. I want to help anyone who is stuck in transition and looking for a breakthrough—the moment when the impossible becomes possible. I will share my life openly and use it as a humble illustration for how transformation is possible. Today I express this desire and calling through my writing as a leadership author, as a transformation speaker and as a certified professional coach. I want to help take people from where they are to where they want to be. There is nothing left for me to preserve and hide and keep for myself. My goal is to *give myself away* to anyone who needs anything I have in order for them to keep moving, keeping striving so they can hit the next level or even just make the next turn.

PIT STOP!

Personal Ramp: What are a few ways you have pretended throughout your life? What are a few ways you could share your vulnerabilities with others today?

____

____

____

____

____

Professional Ramp: How could you expend less energy pretending at work? How would you reallocate your energy in new directions in your work?

____

____

____

____

____

START YOUR TRANSFORMATION WITH *YOU*

I read a quote from Tolstoy recently. "Everyone thinks of changing the world, but no one thinks of changing himself." In the years before the crash, I wanted the world to change, but I never started with myself. I was waiting for change to come to me. And that just doesn't happen, not in a meaningful lasting way.

I'd spent my life doing for others and ignoring myself—picking up the check at dinner, buying the biggest Christmas gifts, being the friend who always showed up first and stayed the longest, then going home and bingeing and overeating pushing off my own needs, ignoring my own worth. My vision was cloudy; I was just going through the motions: waking up, going to work, coming back home, and then doing it all again the next day. But as I took charge of my body and my health, my personal worth leapt up and filled its lungs. I replaced *doing for others* with *doing for me* and, in the process, I replaced food and exhaustion with activity and movement, shame and inadequacy with a true sense of pride and clear marks of personal accomplishment.

I stopped needing to add value to myself by being funny, being smart, being first, and being helpful; I realized that I was and had always been enough—just as I was. And as that realization dawned on me, the protective coating I'd carried from childhood began to burn away. Weight loss was just the beginning. It didn't stop there but expanded into every aspect of who I was.

I STOPPED NEEDING TO ADD VALUE TO MYSELF BY BEING FUNNY, BEING SMART, BEING FIRST, AND BEING HELPFUL; I REALIZED THAT I WAS AND HAD ALWAYS BEEN ENOUGH.

For the first time, I truly realized I was a complete person—and I took that person wherever I went. There was no escaping myself.

Even better, though, I stopped feeling the need to escape. While I'm still learning how to make the best decisions for my life, because I don't always hit the mark, I now have much more certainty about what I will and will not tolerate from people around me, at school, at work, at play, and in life. I am able to spot unhealthy people, unhealthy scenarios, and unhealthy behaviors (even my own) very quickly. When that happens, I pivot; I turn around and go in a new direction.

FOR THE FIRST TIME, I TRULY REALIZED I WAS A COMPLETE PERSON—AND I TOOK THAT PERSON WHEREVER I WENT. THERE WAS NO ESCAPING MYSELF. EVEN BETTER, THOUGH, I STOPPED FEELING THE NEED TO ESCAPE.

The need to add value to yourself is a symptom of a larger issue. If you find that you're trying to add value by actions or words or buying expensive clothes or trips, ask yourself how does it serve? What would happen if you just stopped and focused on yourself? So-called friends and admirers may fall away, but so what? You'll be left with those who truly love you. And if you find you're standing alone, then so be it. Start there and love yourself. You are enough. When you know who you are and what you want, others will stop being greedy about using you up. They'll recognize your boundaries, and they'll start to see you the way you now see yourself.

PIT STOP!

Personal Ramp: What are you doing for others that you're not doing for you? What are you paying attention to in other people but not in yourself?

____

____

____

____

Professional Ramp: In what ways are you trying to please friends or admirers at work?

____

____

____

____

CLEARLY HONEST, ENLIGHTENED LEADERSHIP

Part of getting clear with yourself is learning how to tell yourself the truth. There's clarity, there's being at peace with that clarity, and then there's truthfulness. They're all connected, but when one is lacking, forward motion stops.

Leaders who make an impact know their strengths and weaknesses. They have transparency; they're unafraid to share their confidence and vulnerability, their strengths and weaknesses, with their colleagues and team members. *Enlightened leadership* (which we'll talk about much more later in the book) gives honest feedback (though many leaders shy away from doing so), which helps employees recognize what their own strengths, pitfalls, and blind spots are—and good leaders are willing and able to receive the same sort of feedback themselves. True leadership helps employees see they may be better than they think they are.

When we talk about the wreckage we have in our lives, it covers every aspect of our being. It can be physical wreckage: weight problems or addiction to substances or behaviors; it can be financial wreckage: compulsive spending or debt; it can be home and family wreckage: marital conflict, divorce, or conflict with our children; it may be social wreckage: loneliness or the loss of friendships; and it could be spiritual wreckage: a sense of emptiness or worthlessness. The list goes on and on. We can't run away from the reality of all that wreckage. When we try, we're doomed to repeat the same behaviors until the end of time. We need to tell ourselves the truth: *I am unhealthy. I am overweight. I do not handle my finances well. I drink too much. My most important relationships are a mess. I am self-involved. I treat my friends poorly. I feel hollow inside.* Whatever it is, admit it to yourself! Facing all that negativity might seem like a huge dose of bad news. But the upside is there is an intense power in truthfulness. When wise people say, "The truth will set you free," they aren't kidding.

When I was walking around at my very largest—nearly 350 pounds—I'd tell myself, "Well, I'm a big girl, but I'm still fine. Everyone says I have a pretty face. I'm smart. I get the job done." But the truth was, I wasn't fine. I was morbidly obese, with all the emotional problems and hurt that lies underneath that kind of outward physical symptom. It wasn't until I told myself the truth that I started to deal with the root problem instead of the symptom that showed itself in the numbers on the scales.

It's no different in our professional lives. Not getting promoted? Low sales? Disengaged team? Every single one of those are symptoms. We tell ourselves, "It's not my fault. My boss doesn't like me. No one appreciates the good work I do. I can't break into the inner circle." Lies and *symptoms*. The fact of the matter is such things happen to us due to a lack of preparation. A lack of action. And a definite lack of truth.

WE NEED TO TELL OURSELVES THE TRUTH: I AM UNHEALTHY. I AM OVERWEIGHT. I DO NOT HANDLE MY FINANCES WELL. I DRINK TOO MUCH. MY MOST IMPORTANT RELATIONSHIPS ARE A MESS. I AM SELF-INVOLVED. I TREAT MY FRIENDS POORLY. WHATEVER IT IS, ADMIT IT TO YOURSELF!

So, what if you approached the problems instead of the symptoms. What if you told the truth and said, "I was not ready for that promotion. I was ill prepared for the interview. I didn't show up like I should have. I didn't get my team invested early enough. I micromanaged my team until they no longer had a personal stake in the outcome." There is no shame—the opposite in fact!—in asking yourself what you could have done differently and then taking bold steps to make a change.

PIT STOP!

Personal Ramp: What wreckage do you have in your life that you need to say out loud? What is the toll it's taking on your personal life?

____
____
____
____

Professional Ramp: What role are you *really* ready for? What truth are you not saying about where you are?

____
____
____
____

LIFTING WHILE CLIMBING

As I said before, I often say I sacrifice popularity for effectiveness. Historically, people who are on my team often do quite well, career-wise. There's a reason for that. As their leader, I sit down with them and help them envision, strategize, and execute. I ask them what they want and whether they're ready to hear the truth. If so, I tell them: "Here's what you're really good at. This, not so much. Here are some blind spots and pitfalls for you to keep in mind as you move onward. Let's push! They may not like hearing the truth at that moment—

but what may make them miserable for a short time generally has a positive long-term impact.

For some reason, many work places shy away from a culture of truthfulness in work performance. At HBO, we're known in the industry as being the "nice" company"—and we are. I was lucky to cut my teeth in a place where I was valued and encouraged to grow. My supervisors and colleagues poured goodness and knowledge into me whenever I needed it.

That's all good, but there's a flipside: culturally, many companies are not very forthcoming with performance reviews and observations. This can create an environment where leaders avoid giving the kind of "stronger" feedback that can drive higher-level performance. President James A. Garfield said, "The truth will set you free, but first it will make you miserable." That may be true, but it doesn't let us off the hook. We need to be open to the truth, both to ourselves and hearing it from others. Even negative truth can empower us instead of threaten us.

WHEN I BECAME HONEST WITH MYSELF ABOUT MY OWN STRENGTHS AND WEAKNESSES, I WAS THEN ABLE TO HELP OTHERS BE HONEST ABOUT THEIRS.

When I became honest with myself about my own strengths and weaknesses, I was then able to help others be honest about theirs. As I was growing and expanding, I found I wanted to create a team culture based on honesty—one conducive to growth, development, expansion, and acceleration, not just for me but also for everyone around me.

Several years ago, I had a managerial position open up, and one guy in our office assumed the position would naturally be his. In fact, once I posted it, he stopped by my door and said, "Hey, I don't have to interview for this … it's basically mine, right?"

To his surprise I said, "Well, no. I'm interviewing for this role, so let's set up a time."

Well, in a few weeks after watching a string of people interview for "his" position, he came to me and said, "I just don't know why you're not giving me this job." I knew it was time to have a real honest (not fake honest) conversation. We booked some time to meet in the conference room as I wanted him to be comfortable and in a neutral zone.

I let him know, after speaking to his previous supervisors and coworkers, everyone thought he was incredibly smart and did great work. I also discovered that some colleagues perceived him to have an air of arrogance and a "me" syndrome. I shared with him I was building a new team with a collaborative spirit at the core, and I couldn't risk adding his type of dynamic to the group. No one really wants to work with a "know-it-all."

I watched him turn red. He was clearly disturbed. I asked him, "Does this information and description of you that I'm sharing make sense to you?" As he sat there silently, I explained that I was coming from a place of genuinely wanting to help him and see him progress.

I could see him calm down and begin to take in what I was saying. Then he said, "Yes. I can see it. I just wish someone had told me years ago that I was showing up like that. If I'd known, I could've corrected it. You're the only one who's ever said anything like this to me."

As my literal crash had been for me, that conversation was a *crash moment* for him—and he used it to reassess and turn himself around. After his acknowledgement and more discussion about his true self, I immediately gave him the managerial position, and he went on to become one of the most effective leaders in our company. People began to see him in a new light as his humility rose up and his leadership and intelligence shone through. As this book goes to print, he is now one of the most-championed vice presidents at HBO. He's a great leader—and he's kind enough to credit that conference room meeting with me as the moment that turned everything around for him.

PIT STOP!

Personal Ramp: What are your weaknesses and vulnerabilities?

____

____

____

____

____

Professional Ramp: How do you acknowledge your vulnerabilities in order to give space for others to face theirs?

____

____

____

____

Claiming your personal power—*your* truth—transforms your leadership and actually drives business productivity and work-team efficiency. Once you're *really* honest with yourself and your employees, you'll see change begin to take root as the people around you are inspired to do the same. I believe in lifting while climbing. We all go up together, and as leaders, we need to take the first step ourselves.

I BELIEVE IN LIFTING WHILE CLIMBING. WE ALL GO UP TOGETHER, AND AS LEADERS, WE NEED TO TAKE THE FIRST STEP OURSELVES.

PERSONAL TRANSFORMATION *IS* LEADERSHIP TRANSFORMATION

I discovered I became a better leader once I began to move along my post-crash path of personal enlightenment and self-awareness, and I'm convinced it's the only way for sustainable transformation. You have to acknowledge the wreckage in your life, which has impacted you and helped shape who you are. It's not that there's a way to self-awareness—self-awareness *is* the way. Knowing who you are and accepting yourself in all your flawed and tender glory is what keeps you confident while remaining firm and grounded, allowing you to plant your feet instead of moving and shifting with the wind. It frees you from the opinions of others. It gives you the courage to stand up for justice against bullies. It releases you from having to prove yourself to anyone else. All that insecurity goes out the door once you become intimately knowledgeable about who you are. Best of all, your knowledge transforms your wreckage into power.

I can't say it enough: this lane is the most important. Everything rides on self-knowledge and personal enlightenment. As a leader, how can you help lead others to their greatness if you have yet to discover your own?

I encourage you to start doing that personal inner work—by telling the truth, looking yourself in the eye, imagining the life you want, and writing it down. By affirming the life you want each day, you will start to see shifts happen. Wreckage may shape you, but it doesn't define you. See where you want to go and you'll get there. It works. It really does.

Today I know that whatever capacity or role I play: entry level sales trainer, Director in distribution, VP of recruiting, VP of sales strategy, author, speaker, coach, friend, sister, auntie, etc. there is a possibility that any part of my story may impact someone enough to move in a new, more positive direction. I'm also realizing I don't have to be perfect to do this. I, too, am on this road of life, learning and collecting information to make myself better each mile and sharing those new findings as well, no matter how vulnerable it makes me.

The moment we believe we have to be perfect before we can help someone then we've missed the point of life. Momma told us long ago no one was put on this earth for themselves. We're all here to support, encourage and help one another … somehow, someway.

PIT STOP!

Personal Ramp: What wreckage has shaped your make and model?

____

____

____

____

____

____

Professional Ramp: How does your make and model cause you to show up at work?

____

____

____

____

____

____

LANE 2

"DONE IS BETTER THAN PERFECT."

—ANONYMOUS

PUNCH IN YOUR DESTINATION

I have some big news for you. Most people believe it's the journey, not the destination, that counts. I want to challenge the consensus. Having a sense of direction or, even better, knowing exactly what you want ("*See Rome*") gets you to your destination faster.

To me, journeys often imply drifting or taking a wandering path, going with the flow. Don't get me wrong. There will certainly be "pull off the road" moments—but how quickly you refocus and get back *on* the road is what counts. Be vigilant about where you want to go, and believe in yourself enough to keep your foot on the gas, not just coast or hover over the brakes. That's how you get there.

Once you are able to start practicing this "drive to goal" in your personal life then it shows up everywhere else, especially at work. And it'll show up in your leadership, which is about knowing and communicating the desired destination—and then encouraging your team to find the best ways to get there.

PROGRESS, NOT PERFECTION

Here's something else I say a lot: "It's about progression not perfection." Perfection doesn't have to be the goal. In fact, if perfection is your goal, stop now; it won't happen. I tried it. Seeking perfection actually creates more anxiety than accomplishment. If you can take one step in the direction of where you want to go, that's better than no step, even if you don't get all the way to your goal the first time. In fact, you can even take a wrong turn here and there. In the long run, a wrong turn can be the right move—as long as you learn from it and grow.

As humans, we learn and grow by making mistakes, then correcting course and improving. As a leader, conveying this to your team helps them to relax so they can take risks and take responsibility for their own choices and forward movement. If you demand perfection all the time every time, your employees learn that taking a risk and making a mistake, no matter how small, is unacceptable. By demanding perfection, you are hamstringing their progress and infantilizing your workforce. You want your employees moving, growing, reaching—not static and waiting for everything to fall into place so they can please you.

Companies with a high perfectionism culture are very bureaucratic, hierarchical, and procedure oriented. Before you have the meeting to decide if there's going to be a meeting, fifteen people have to approve the meeting and the agenda, and then add their comments and corrections. The drive for perfection actually creates tension between departments and groups. This kind of thinking and behavior is slow and nitpicky. It strips people of their desire to strive individually for the good of the group by making their own choices.

WE CAN ACCEPT WORK THAT IS GOOD ENOUGH—AS LONG AS IT'S GOOD ENOUGH TO KEEP THINGS MOVING FORWARD, ROLLING AHEAD.

I'm going to take a radical step here and say that we can accept work that is good enough—as long as it's good enough to keep things moving forward, rolling ahead. Sometimes "good enough" might look a lot like "perfect," but most of the time it's just that—good enough to keep going. Typos in an internal e-mail? Don't waste time fixing them all. Hit send. If you got your message across, that's good enough. You fulfilled the purpose of the e-mail, which I'm assuming was to convey information, not to show everyone that you're a perfect speller.

Before my crash moment, I was a big perfectionist. It makes sense when I think about it now. I didn't have control over the most important things in my personal life, the intangibles, so I took control over things that I could touch, feel, and do. Completing assignments, delivering projects, executing plans, and even writing email flawlessly were my top concerns. Because I didn't "look" perfect I had to make everything else perfect. I drove my teams crazy back then. You see how low self-esteem and low self-awareness in my personal life negatively impacted my work life and my leadership. It's all connected. Of course, I still have to catch myself sometimes about wanting something to be just right—but the operative phrase here is *catch myself.* The room isn't set up perfectly for my presentation? Let's work with it. My computer stops working just before my conference call? It's cool. Someone—possibly myself—made a mistake in the report? Let's fix it, learn from it, and keep moving.

It's one thing to seek a high level of quality and take pride in that, but remember that perfection is a static thing. Once you reach it, there is nowhere left to go. Instead, why not focus on growth, on innovation, on development and forward motion? If you're going to be honest about how to accomplish those things, you'd better be ready to throw perfection out the window. Once you do, progress will come welling up to fill the vacant space. Because the good news is you don't have to be perfect to be fantastic.

Letting go of the perfection deception starts in your personal sphere. I'm not advocating that you let your house go to the dogs, but I will say you can have a streak on your window or a hole in your sock and still be a good person, worthy of love. That may sound obvious, but it's amazing how many of us quietly hold those beliefs of inadequacy as a truth deep down in our subconscious.

As you let go of impossible expectations in your own life, bring that same process into the workplace. As a leader, don't be afraid to share your progress—or your ideas for progress in the company—with your employees. Instead of top-down leadership, try leadership with the top down. (Life's always better in a convertible, right?) Remove your impossible expectations for perfection and focus instead on growth and progress. Let your team know you are open to their ideas (or at least you're *learning* to be more open to their ideas), and let them know how best to present those ideas to you. Give them confidence that if a better idea than your own comes along, you're going to implement it. No matter who it comes from, regardless of the department, the seniority, or the level of pay, the best idea in the room always wins! Tell your team you're going to be upfront with them about what you know—and what you don't know.

INSTEAD OF TOP-DOWN LEADERSHIP, TRY LEADERSHIP WITH THE TOP DOWN. (LIFE'S ALWAYS BETTER IN A CONVERTIBLE, RIGHT?)

As you gain confidence and your team grows stronger, you'll be ready to do the bravest thing a leader can do and we've all heard it before: start hiring people who are smarter than you are or even just plain better at some things. Hire people who are more talented or who have more experience with things you're not very good at. I work with team members now who are much smarter than I am in many areas. You're not there to be the smartest person in the room; you just need to be the best *leader* in the room.

No matter what we do, eventually we'll make a mistake. Something will block our way. It's inevitable. Perfection just isn't possible. But if you understand how you're connected to the people around you—and how you got to where you are now—you stand to benefit from those crash moments. So, be ready for them when they come. Make something out of them that will be far better than the "perfection" you thought was your goal.

PIT STOP!

Personal Ramp: In what ways is perfectionism holding you back in your day-to-day life?

____

____

____

____

Professional Ramp: What does focusing on the learning and growing of your team members—rather than demanding perfection—look like to you on a daily basis? How is that focus different than focusing on perfection?

____

____

____

____

DON'T HOG THE WHEEL

There's another phrase I use at work. "Leadership is not just for leaders." I believe in leadership from every seat. Everyone has a contribution to make and *should* be contributing to our common goal. Everyone should be involved in designing the playbook of how best to get there. Everyone. Making sure that happens is *why you're here.*

When I was head of recruiting for HBO two years ago, I would tell my team, "Listen. I don't look for you all to just come into work each day and hang your brain up with your coat. I not only want you engaged in what we're doing for the company strategically and initiative-wise, I actually want you to help carve a new path forward. I want you to help me—us, our team, this business unit—begin to design what new profiles of successful candidates will look like. I want to hear your thoughts and ideas for new talent attraction strategies."

I BELIEVE IN LEADERSHIP FROM EVERY SEAT. EVERYONE HAS A CONTRIBUTION TO MAKE AND *SHOULD* BE CONTRIBUTING TO OUR COMMON GOAL.

Our recruiting team is proactive, involved and on the lookout for top talent, the best people. We worked together with the business to create and design prototypes of ideal candidates before positions were even open. These prototypes helped us guide applicants into positions who were the best fit for their talents and gifts, so when a hiring manager said, "I need an analyst in such-and-such department," we are already ready to hit the ground running.

We amassed the knowledge to create those profiles, *not* by relying on just my experience and decision-making abilities, but by pooling the knowledge and experience of the entire team—and then taking it to the departments. We wove in our social networks, as well as conversations outside of work, and then brought all that data back home and crafted strategic approaches to the best of our ability.

Here's an example of what we did when my assistant brought a great idea to the table. She came in one morning and said, "Carla, I was talking to one of my dear friends who was just hired at a consulting firm, and when she walked in on her first day, her name was written in lights in the lobby." It was a simple idea—the names of new hires were cast on the wall with one of those light-beam projectors saying, "Welcome so-and-so!"

At that point, I'd only been in recruiting for a year. Until then, I'd spent my entire career in the domestic distribution part of our company, the revenue-generating part of our business. After many years there I was known for building high-performance work teams quickly. When there was an opportunity to bring my brand of leadership into a department that could potentially impact other business units and help build other teams, I jumped at the chance.

Because of who I am and how I do things, I wanted my impact to exceed my new department's expectations. To do that, I knew I would need a team that could explore, embody, and execute the unique, innovative strategies and techniques happening in talent acquisition—and bring them to HBO. I even wanted them to explore small ideas so we could log "small wins" in order to feel our progress. Small wins also keep people from being overwhelmed and intimidated by such new and lofty goals (like asking them to help shape and build their own new recruiting department).

When my assistant shared the idea about putting new hire names in lights on their first day at work, the team got the ball rolling, saying, "Not only can we do this here—we can do it better!"

The brainstorming took off from there. In the HBO lobby in New York, there's a large television monitor next to the elevators, almost as wide as the wall. We use it to promote things, such as our own leadership announcements, upcoming events and training sessions in the building. So we started saying to each other, "Imagine if we did something with that giant TV—a screenshot that said "Welcome New Hires, You've Been Cast! James Smith—Accounting Manager, Maggie Jones—Sales Analyst, Derek Williams—Custodial Manager, etc."

After all, who doesn't want to see their name in lights and hear they've been cast in the role of a lifetime? We wanted to reinforce the excitement people feel when they start their career at HBO. Most people who work for us have a passion for our programming and the industry in general. Those fantastic movies, shows, and documentaries couldn't exist without every one of us at the company doing our part.

Excited to see her idea taking shape, my assistant asked, "Can I put it together?"

I said, "This is *your* project. Run with it!"

Within three weeks, we had the new-hire welcome greeting on the lobby monitor and then launched it nationally on our HBO intranet. Everyone loved it! Every two weeks, new employee names go up with their job titles alongside images of our hit shows.

This may have been a small idea—but it was a big win. It made my assistant know she was a critical part of our team's forward motion. It showed the team they really can have an idea come to life. And for leaders, championing someone else's idea is a great way to build creative momentum. It drives the spirit of innovation and proves that your words are true and real.

The beauty of this approach is that it creates a living, breathing organism, capable of regenerating itself. I'm there guiding and encouraging, making the tough decisions that have to be made. In return, the culture in the department makes a shift, whether big or small. People will shift. When you allow people a voice, not only do they feel like they add value and know why they are in their job, but they also see they are endorsed and supported and they are important. We all need that!

PIT STOP!

Personal Ramp: What parts of your personal/family life do you try to control or micromanage? How could accepting any kind of help and advice from others improve your life and relationships? If you were to let go of control or stop micromanaging, what would that look like?

____

____

____

____

Professional Ramp: How often do you encourage others to share their ideas and input at work? How might you invite others to "take the wheel" on a current project?

____

____

____

FLASH YOUR BRIGHTS: ENLIGHTENED LEADERSHIP

The quickest way to make people love their job is to introduce freedom into the atmosphere. Freedom breeds creativity. It gives people room to think, to wonder, to find new paths forward. People bring their whole selves to work—and what more could a manager want? If someone is creative and likes to draw, design, or write, I want to tap into that.

We all want to know that we matter. It's fundamental. So, leaders, why not validate that we are working side by side with real people? Why not embrace the wholeness of our team members? Not just their accounting degree, but the fact they're an accountant *and* they love event planning? Perhaps that creativity can be used to support an additional function for the team. Create an environment that's conducive to making people want to bring different parts of themselves to the table.

Enlightened leaders know who they are and what they are here for; they no longer feel a need to compete and prove how good they are. Instead of showing the world how good *they* are, enlightened leaders help other people discover how good others *can be.*

We all have a unique talent or gift, something we were given to share with the world. Leaders should realize the forty or fifty hours a week people spend at work is the perfect opportunity for people to deliver on the promise of their talents and gifts. Enlightened leaders strive to bring people together in creative ways to let their talents flow and bubble up to the top.

So many leaders are focused on their own worth, their own achievement, their own advancement—they forget they're actually there to lead, not to rule. When you're self-focused, even your own growth is stifled. Eventually, you will be replaced. If you're the person holding back all the amazing people from doing their thing and great people keep leaving your department, somebody is going to notice. And if they don't, it will still catch up with you because people won't give you their best. You're better than that. And so are your coworkers and team members.

The people on your team are human beings with passions, interests, dreams, and goals. Sometimes their dreams align perfectly with what they're doing on the job and sometimes they are there to do a job, take home their paycheck, and get health insurance so they can pursue their passions in their free time. But what would happen if you were able to bring their talents and passions to the forefront and integrate them into their work lives?

PIT STOP!

Personal ramp: What can you do today to encourage others to use their gifts to achieve a common goal, both at work and in your personal life?

____

____

____

____

Professional Ramp: Do you know if your team members have particular talents? Get to know their talents and encourage them to share and use those regularly.

____

____

____

____

"EXPECT MORE FROM YOURSELF THAN OTHERS. EXPECTATION FROM OTHERS MAY HURT YOU WHILE EXPECTING MORE FROM YOURSELF WILL INSPIRE YOU A LOT."

—RYAN FERRERAS

CHANGE YOUR OWN TIRES

Great leaders understand where they've been and where they want to be. They have an innate sense that something better awaits them, and they believe in their ability to achieve it. When roadblocks delay their progress or require them to reroute the path, successful leaders don't just give up—they confidently put a plan in place that allows them to get back on the road. When facing challenges and setbacks, real leaders push through and remain intent on arriving at their desired destination.

A NEW PLACE, A NEW YOU

In my hometown of Centerville, Tennessee, I'd created a safe place where people liked me *despite* my shortcomings, at least, that's how

I perceived it. Over the first eighteen years of my life, I'd won them over by proving I was someone worth including. With college on the horizon, though, I realized I was going to have to start all over again. No one would know me, no one would love me; to them, I'd just be another overweight, dark-skinned, small-town girl clutching her books to her chest and walking alone to class. *Overweight, dark, small-town*—those were labels I'd given myself, and unless I let them go, they were going to follow me wherever I went.

Being brand new to a place—whether it's a city, a company, a role, or even a party where you don't know anyone—forces you to find a way to connect and establish who you are. For me, this first launch into the world was the signature point in my life where I went from being protected in Centerville to figuring out who I was, who I wanted to be, and what mark I'd make on the world. I knew where I'd come from—but who would I become? I knew consciously I wanted to be different from who I was when I woke up in Centerville. I wanted to be stronger, to have a clearer point of view. I didn't really know what all that entailed, but I knew that there was another level to my life, a deeper direction I wanted to go. I went to college with this small bit of clarity in my mind.

FUEL FOR THOUGHT

Warning: Be careful of the labels you give yourself because they define who you are. Labels can propel you forward or hold you back.

LESSONS IN SELF-RELIANCE

My mother is one of the smartest women I know, and she modeled leadership by teaching us to be responsible for ourselves, whether that meant knowing how to do our laundry or knowing where to find information to expand our minds. She wanted us to be successful when she pushed us out of the nest. It wasn't enough to *have* wings, we had to know how to flap them, too.

Momma made sure we were equipped for the wider world. She was smart about it in many ways. For example, she knew that, culturally, many African-Americans don't know how to swim, she had us in swimming lessons at an early age. She had a sixth sense that knowing how to swim was a literal and figurative metaphor that would open up the world to us and give us opportunities; it would open doors instead of shutting them. A few years ago an HBO show featured a story on how black children are three times more likely to die by drowning than any other ethnic group, simply because swimming is not typically a skill valued or taught in black families. Historically, we didn't have access to pools. Momma did not want that to be us. She wanted us to be able to go wherever we wanted, and she wanted to eliminate our fears wherever she could—whether that was the university of our choice or the deep end of the pool.

MOMMA WANTED US TO BE ABLE TO GO WHEREVER WE WANTED, AND SHE WANTED TO ELIMINATE OUR FEARS WHEREVER SHE COULD

One day when I was around eight years old, there was a knock at the door. There on our front step was a salesman peddling Childcraft and the World Book Encyclopedia door to door, as they did back then. We did not have money to spend like that, but I distinctly remember Momma counting out what we did have, then asking the man to put us on a payment plan. She was an avid reader (and salutatorian of her high school class, I proudly add), and the minute she laid her eyes on these book collections, she knew instinctively that having a set of our own was going to open our minds. And she was right.

As kids, we put Momma and Daddy under a constant barrage of questions. "Is Timbuktu a real place?" "What does Africa look like?" "Do Eskimos really live in igloos?" "Is the North Pole a place with reindeer, or is that all made up?"

No matter the question, Momma would turn to us and say, "Go look it up in the World Book. Go see what you can find out."

Before the Internet, those books were our go-to manuals of comprehensive intelligence. And because of the way we touched so many pages as we flipped to the section we wanted, they taught us in a way the Internet never could. Smelling the paper as the spine cracked, opening to a favorite passage on explorers or native tribes of Africa or dodo birds or whatever it was that struck our fancy, those Childcraft and World Books did just what Momma had anticipated. We were lost in them, those beautifully bright and colorful pictures and words. We traveled the world through them. We met children from Bangladesh and Holland and saw cement trucks and skyscrapers.

Lying on the living room floor, browsing the section about Italy, a crisp page of the World Book is where I first "saw" Rome. I stared at those ruins as a thousand bells went off in my brain. This place existed BC! I had to go there one day. I had to see it for myself.

Momma did more than just encourage us to swim, read, and otherwise expand our horizons; she also made sure to teach us practical skills that would help us become productive adults. The year before I headed to college, she made me wake myself up for school on time with my own alarm clock, cook my own food, and do my own laundry. She made sure I was ready to be on my own.

Momma used to say this Bible quote all the time: "Train up a child in the way he should go and when he is old he will not depart from it." Of course, when talking to the girls she would replace "he" with "she." Little did we know then but Momma was giving us insights on how to raise our own children (my niece and nephews). "You only know you've raised a child properly when he or she goes out into the world." Thank you Momma.

PIT STOP!

Personal Ramp: What did you learn at an early age that today allows you to explore and expand your life? Do you tap into this knowledge regularly? What did this early knowledge teach you or expose you to?

____

____

____

____

Professional Ramp: How can you rely less on others at work to answer questions or provide support and be more proactive and self-reliant today? How can you encourage your team members to build and rely on their own efforts and abilities?

____

____

____

____

PROVING TO YOURSELF THAT YOU CAN DO IT

Before I left for college Momma told me, "I prepared you to do what you need to do to be successful, and now it's time to take what's been given to you and go do it."

I'd never been on my own, but I knew I was going to make it. I can still hear myself thinking, *I may not know where English class is tomorrow, and I'm going to have to ask fifteen people as I move across campus because this place is about as big as the entire town of Centerville. And—oh my gosh!—how am I going to get around from building to building from class to class on time?! I don't even know where these buildings are!* But I found my way. I navigated. I asked for help and surrendered to the process.

I grew up in college, as most people do. It's not just about what you learn in the classroom. I learned life skills, from how to cook a grilled-cheese sandwich with an iron and a brown paper bag (Daddy gave me that tip) to how to budget and stretch my academic scholarship stipend from here to kingdom come … or at least until the first of each month. I learned to be resourceful and to rely on myself to cover the basics. Money didn't come from home each month—we didn't always have that luxury—so I knew it was up to me to make things work.

The number of students on Middle Tennessee State University's campus was literally quadruple the size of my hometown, but I found my way. And then I began to *make* my way. The lessons I learned in those first days were to reach out, ask for help, and get involved. You can choose to stay in darkness—or you can actively seek the light. I aimed for the sun.

And as I started to find my own sense of belonging, I became finely attuned to those who were in need of help. This idea of connecting, engaging, pulling other people into your world so that you can offer a hand was something that I began to reinforce and strengthen. We learned that at home. As I became stronger, I wanted to help others move through that darkness a little more quickly. In turn, I gained a stronger community around me. As mentioned in Lane 1, I call this *lifting while climbing* and it factors heavily in my mentoring and leadership style today.

PIT STOP!

Personal Ramp: What early-growth opportunities have you benefited from most in your personal life? And those from more recently?

____

____

____

____

Professional Ramp: How can you lift while climbing at work? Who have you noticed being in need, and how might you offer assistance or mentorship?

____

____

____

____

IF YOU DON'T PUSH YOURSELF, WHO WILL?

As I've mentioned, my weight was out of control before my accident. When I had a hard day, I'd say, "Have an ice cream, Carla. You deserve it." When I did well, I'd say, "Pizza tonight, Carla, we're celebrating." I thought I was being good to myself, but the fact is, I was being *easy* on myself. I was easy on myself to the tune of nearly three hundred pounds. It wasn't until I was hard on myself that things started to turn around in my favor.

Most people these days will tell you, "Give yourself a break! You're only human!" But I've found many people are *too* easy on themselves. I think we see the most growth and progress when we make really hard choices and stick with them. It's widely understood now that growth happens outside your comfort zone. Of course, the world outside your comfort zone is—surprise, surprise—uncomfortable! Being able to constantly exist outside your comfort zone requires a level of mental toughness that most people find challenging. Heck, I did! It's one thing to give yourself a moment to recuperate after a hard day—but if you allow yourself too many breaks, you quickly lose momentum and focus.

When we talk about transformation, we are talking about movement. You will not be in the same place at the end of a transformation as you were at the beginning. This really came to life for me the day I checked in for my first triathlon, a women-only race. So many ladies were wearing t-shirts with the slogan, "The woman who starts a triathlon is the not the same woman who finishes it." I didn't really know what that meant … until the next day. I think I came in next to last in that race but certainly remember the feeling. It was true. I was one woman when I started at sunbreak at the river's edge in my pink swim cap (for the older set) and was someone different running through the tape hours later. I felt the difference. A new strength, a sense of power, an honoring of and belief in myself. Realizing I had gone from 300 pounds to triathlete knocked me to my knees in joy. We don't know what that place will look like because we haven't been there yet. That sense of "not knowing" holds most people back from making any kind of significant change, even when all signs point to the certainty that things will be *better* once the change is complete! You have to go for it!

Think of it this way, if Michelangelo had stopped sculpting *David* when things got hard, if he had spent countless hours consoling himself with espresso and wine, then all the world would have today would be a lump of busted marble. What you're doing and what you're working on may be frustrating, but until it's finished, you won't know how it will alter your life.

Here's the thing: the harder it is, the more likely your breakthrough is just around the corner. The closer you are, the harder it gets. That's just the way it is. I've learned to use that as a marker. When something's getting harder and harder, most people will back off and retreat—but that is exactly when you want to push. It's that *stick-to-itiveness* that makes the difference between good and great.

As you push through toward greatness, you're going to get some blowback. Not everyone is going to like you all the time. Not everyone is going to see the potential in you. You just have to feel it, to know it for yourself, because, ultimately, when the knocks come—and they will—you're the one who will have to stand back up and shout for more. Remember, transformation means you aren't going to stay the same; you are going to be something different.

FUEL FOR THOUGHT

Who you are at work is who you are inside. You have to get that piece shored up so you can be your full self at work. If we're not fully who we are, then we cannot fully be in the world.

PIT STOP!

Personal Ramp: What will you do today, right now, to set your sights on the horizon and drive beyond your comfort zone? What is your lump of busted marble: an unmet goal, or an unfinished project? How can you complete it so others can discover and enjoy it?

Professional Ramp: What can you do at work that is uncomfortable: a risk you could take on that you wouldn't normally—something to stretch you and benefit others?

THERE'S NO WHINING IN LEADERSHIP

Most people don't realize it's the difficulty of a journey that prepares you for the destination. For example, if you want a top job title and you don't have a difficult journey to get there, then you may not be able to handle the job that comes with the title. Most roads are not straight, and most journeys require planning, preparation, and perseverance—and that last one may be the hardest.

I've come across many, many people who want to be promoted at work but have yet to turn in one assignment their boss didn't ask them to deliver. People who do not offer innovative ideas, take initiative, or go above and beyond are not seen as having leadership potential. They want to arrive at their desired destination without doing any of the planning and preparation—in fact, they don't even want to do the driving!

FUEL FOR THOUGHT

When you don't build strength during your journey, your crash moments become your defining moments. I live strongly and boldly today because my journey was so difficult. If I hadn't got tough along the way, I wouldn't be here today. Living through the wreckage results in a refined, powerful version of you.

Often in job interviews, I ask people, "What was the last project you worked on without having been told to do so?"

They look at me, confused, and say, "What do you mean?" I always know that's a bad sign! I'm looking for proactive future leaders—people who have vision and move on it.

When you don't expect higher from your employees, you weaken the team. Don't accept complacency or whining in your workplace—accept action! If someone doesn't like your mission or agenda, let them know they're welcome to present alternative ideas of their own ... but they are not, under any circumstance, allowed to whine about it. Whining and pouting and complaining will get you nowhere, not in baseball, and certainly not in leadership.

IF SOMEONE DOESN'T LIKE YOUR MISSION OR AGENDA, LET THEM KNOW THEY'RE WELCOME TO PRESENT ALTERNATIVE IDEAS OF THEIR OWN ... BUT THEY ARE NOT, UNDER ANY CIRCUMSTANCE, ALLOWED TO WHINE ABOUT IT. WHINING AND POUTING AND COMPLAINING WILL GET YOU NOWHERE, NOT IN BASEBALL, AND CERTAINLY NOT IN LEADERSHIP.

Life isn't always going to be lollipops and rainbows. Your ideas are not always going to be accepted ... and neither are you! You're likely to run into people who are downright gunning for you. But having the capacity to absorb criticism, listen to feedback, and gracefully weather scenarios that are not ideal will add up. As you flex your mental toughness, other people will begin to see you as the one who gets things done instead of complaining. And your team will thank you.

PIT STOP!

Personal Ramp: Do you know how to change your own tires? Literally? If not, learn how, then share that knowledge with someone else. What are three other things you can learn and share with others to foster your leadership transformation?

____

____

____

____

Professional Ramp: What are three things you and your team can learn and share, or three actions you can do to help you arrive at your desired destination?

____

____

____

____

LANE 4

"DON'T LOOK BACK, YOU'RE NOT GOING THAT WAY."

—MARY ENGELBREIT

SHIFT FROM JUNKYARD TO SHOWROOM

The beauty and strength of one inspires many. The beauty and strength of many elevates the world.

I've always believed in moving and growing and bringing others along with me. It's that "lifting while climbing" approach. As I grow, I want to bring people up—to show off their talents and help them along the way. That's just true for me in my personal life as it is in my professional life. After all, like I said earlier: one self, one life. There is truly no divide. The more I begin to learn growth and development strategies and see the effect they have in my life, the more I want to teach these same practices and principals to others so they can enjoy the benefits in their own lives. Personal growth and effective leadership go hand-in-hand.

STALLED DREAMS

While college is where I learned to stand on my own, it's also where I learned what it felt like to be beaten down ... then rise up strong again. Things were going well for me, at least academically and socially. I was enjoying my classes. I had a great group of friends. I was hoping to pledge a sorority. I'd been elected dorm president my sophomore year and led our dorm to a homecoming competition victory. I was calling on my creativity and living out the dream I'd had back when I ran for Beta Club President in Centerville: to touch, connect, engage, and inspire others. I was on my way to being *me*.

Record scratch.

At the same time, I was still gaining weight, and I had never addressed the reasons why. As I gained skills in one area, I piled on pounds in another. (I bring up my weight so often because I was defined by it from early childhood right up until my crash moment. And because I'm honest, it still plays a major part in the script of my life.)

There were so many things I couldn't do because of my size, so many things I didn't feel I had the *right* to do. When you're overweight, you often walk through life feeling like you should apologize to everyone you meet for the fact that you can't control your own body. How can you stand up and ask people to take you seriously when you can't even control what goes in your mouth? It's an emotional and creative drain, in addition an exhausting physical state.

Well, I came up against that in college when I finally found myself in a situation where being smart and fun and helpful and friendly didn't matter. I couldn't cheer my way out of this one. My weight was front and center.

I'd chosen to major in radio/TV broadcasting. Why? Because I just *knew* I was going to be the next six o'clock news anchor in Nashville, Tennessee. I picked MTSU for its Mass Communications program; it's known for having the best communications program in the South.

So, freshman year, I walked into Communications 101, and just like that five-year-old Carla you met in Lane 1, I sat down and surveyed my surroundings. It was a massive lecture hall filled with hundreds of other hopefuls. But I was there. I was me. And I was going to succeed.

About a month into the class, however, our instructor said something that was the exact opposite of "lifting while climbing." He said, "Not everyone in this room is going to make it in broadcasting. Not everyone is going to be an anchor on TV. You have to have a certain *level of attractiveness* to be in front of the camera in this business. If you don't, you will not make it. That's just the cold, hard facts—the cold-hearted truth."

I knew I could still do it, because at that point, Oprah had just come to TV and I thought to myself, "Well, she's big, she's on TV, she was a news reporter, she was a broadcaster." I looked at Oprah as beautiful and powerful, but back then, other people didn't always see her that way. I saw her as someone to aspire to be like, someone to lead the way.

But in that echoing auditorium, with my instructor's words hanging in the air, he seemed to be talking about me—*just me*—and not the other three hundred people sitting there with me. I felt as though he was trying to send me a message. I went back to my dorm room and cried my eyes out. I let the walls fall down around me—then I picked myself up and changed my major to Public Relations and Marketing. I couldn't get past his words. I was too insecure. Besides, he was an expert! He was our teacher! He would know … right?

PIT STOP!

Personal Ramp: The negative influences of others is often not obvious, not in-your-face. What are some of the silent influencers you're seeing now in your personal sphere? How do these silent influencers affect your self-esteem at home and in life?

____

____

____

____

____

Professional Ramp: The corporate landscape is a high-competition, low-trust environment. Relationships change as positions change and people protect themselves. The person who helped you last year may hinder you this year. How can you not allow non-supporters to keep you stagnant? How can you work around their disbelief in you?

____

____

____

____

____

STEPPING ONTO THE SHOWROOM FLOOR

Come spring, the end of my freshman year, I was well into my new public-relations and marketing coursework when I decided to be a resident assistant. Not only do you get your own dorm room if you're an RA, it's often a big room. The whole space was my own. I loved the privacy, and it taught me how to live alone and be with myself. Quiet if I wanted, music if I wanted, time to sit with my own thoughts if I wanted. I loved this part of my life.

That summer, instead of going home, I stayed with my brother and his wife in Nashville. I wanted to work, shop, hang out, and live life outside of college but not at home. Being with my brother was big fun always. It was a golden summer, the three of us spending time together on our own, getting to know each other outside the dynamics of our family back in Centerville. That summer remains as one the most favorite times of my life. My brother taught me a lot, especially about self-reliance. I'll never forget after my first month with them he asked for rent money. I said, "What? I have to pay you to live here?"

He said, "Once you're grown, ain't nothing free. You have to take care of yourself." Those were his exact words and they helped shape me today.

One week before school started, I went back for RA training. Many of us were studying communications or broadcasting, so on the last day, they made us take everything we learned and put it into a skit. They divided up the room and my group had enough people to create an Oprah show. And—dream of dreams!—I was Oprah.

Back then, Oprah would run through the audiences, jumping over people to ask them questions, with her scarf flying everywhere. She was actively engaged with the people in the audience. Our breakout group was large enough that we had an audience and panelists. And I, of course, had the mic and the scarf. Ha! So I dove in, acting like Oprah, running around taking questions from the audience about the campus, about registering for classes, about dorm life—whatever came up, I was on it. The room hollered, and we had a ball that day. But little did I know, in the audience was the news producer for the school television channel.

After it was over, he came up to me and said, "Carla, you need your own show."

I was flabbergasted. "Are you kidding me? I've been wanting to be on TV forever. What do you mean? What are you talking about?"

"You need your own talk show," he said. "We'll call it *The Carla Moore Show*. And we'll run it out of the university production studio."

I believe that every step I've taken, and every level that I've reached, personally and professionally, was a direct result of people reaching out to help. Number one, I believe they saw in me someone who was humble and hungry for an opportunity, who absolutely knew how to appreciate help. I knew how to honor and respect help because I knew that help was a gift! I didn't look at it as something bad. I knew that everything given to me was in service to a larger purpose.

And so, the university news producer lifted me up, and just like that, in the first semester of my sophomore year, *The Carla Moore Show* was born. We taped each show complete with a live studio audience, guest panelists, the works. The show was broadcast throughout Murfreesboro and the surrounding areas. Even some places in Nashville could get the show. We shot once a week, then twice a week. It got to where the show was popular enough I became somewhat recognizable—not only on campus but in town, as well.

At that point, my work-study job wasn't bringing in enough money, so I took a job as a cashier at Long John Silver's. My brother made me a hustler! I was filming, going to class, doing my homework, doing my work-study job, and then on weekends, it was, "Welcome to Long John Silver's. Would you like a two-piece Fish and More?" Even in my full yellow and blue visor and uniform, people started coming up to me and saying, "I know you! I've seen you on TV! Are you Carla Moore?" I'd smile and say, "Yes, it's me."

Then things started to get crazy. I didn't have professional clothes to wear, but a woman's clothing store called the station saying they'd like to send me some nice clothes in exchange for credit and acknowledgment at the end of the show. Then people wanted to be on my show. Students wrote in asking, "How can I get on the show? How can I be a panelist?" I made the front page of the school newspaper, then the city newspaper. They called me "Murfreesboro's Oprah." It was a high time in my life.

Just an aside, if anyone reading this has footage of *The Carla Moore Show,* please let me know. I would love to see those tapes! The reason those tapes would mean so much to me now is because of what they represent. Now that I'm back working in television, the river of my life has returned to its natural course.

After I had allowed one teacher to make me feel not good enough, here was the whole community saying he was wrong. Succeeding on that show was my way to defy judgment of my worth, to reclaim my confidence, no matter what my size was.

I began to blossom, to really champion causes, and I started to integrate community service into my life and mission—from becoming a leader in Pi Sigma Epsilon, a premiere marketing fraternity, to my public service work through Delta Sigma Theta Sorority, Inc., to my church and beyond. Momma always had us doing public service, and I understood how organizations worked—and now I had a platform for change. Everything was moving me toward what would happen next. I took out that beat-up, broken-down model, polished it up, and drove it out on the showroom floor.

PIT STOP!

Personal Ramp: When has someone in your personal life lifted you up by offering you help? How did you respond? After this experience, do you ask more for help?

____

____

____

____

____

____

Professional Ramp: Recall a "showroom" moment in your career. Who helped you get there? At the time, did you honor their help? Or did you respond with discomfort, embarrassment, or some other emotion?

____

____

____

____

____

____

RUNNING AT TOP CAPACITY

Imagine if all the people you know—even ones you don't know—were operating at their highest level of self. What would the world look like? What could we accomplish if everyone was truly running at top capacity? It's beyond comprehension how wonderful it would be. You already possess the power within you to change your very own life; when you do, even if you make small changes to improve your life, the ripple effect can be astounding.

When we bring that transformative power into the workplace, the ripple effects can quickly change the culture and work community, then spill out into the personal lives of the people affected. I once heard "The only time you should be looking down at someone is if you're also reaching out a hand to lift them up." This is how we should approach the personal and professional growth of our team members and employees—and everyone around us, really.

Of course, no one is going to follow your lead if you're walking in the shadows. You've got to get yourself together first. Dust yourself off, start making the big fixes, then reach out and start helping your team members to become the best *they* can be.

There is a great fear among many leaders in corporate America that lifting an employee up too far will overshadow the leader; you want them to do well, but not *too* well. Rather than surrounding themselves with bright and shiny showroom models, these leaders park themselves in the middle of junkyard models, downplaying others' talents and successes to make sure they're the shiniest car on the lot.

When you do this—when you keep other people down so you can be the only showroom-worthy model—it doesn't end up having the effect you think it will. Instead of looking extra shiny, you'll just look bright and pompous surrounded by a bunch of junkers. But polish up those models and get them into top condition, and you're the miracle worker who found the hidden gems that were there all along.

I've learned the brighter your team shines, the clearer it is what kind of leader you really are.

My goal is to get you showroom ready. Whatever that is for you, I want you to have it. I want you to achieve it. But as soon as you're ready, I want you to challenge, encourage, and even *push* the rest of your team into being showroom ready, too. That will mean different things to different people on your staff. You may find some very stable Hondas and Subarus that will be with you for the long haul, but you may also find that you've got a few new Ferraris and Lamborghinis suddenly primed and revving their engines. That can be intimidating. But remember—you are there to LEAD, not to shine the brightest. To *lead.*

Sometimes, being a great leader means knowing when to let another car pull ahead and pass or move on down another road. It takes a lot of courage and firm sense of self to allow people to be their best—to allow them to move past you if that's their destiny, or to accelerate at a speed that seems unfair, based on your own ascent. Take a breath, and remember we're all on our own path, have our own purpose, and work to reach our own full potential as others continue to reach theirs. It will not hurt you in the long run. Instead, you'll become known for turning out incredible finds and putting the health of the company and the team first, which is what a leader ought to be doing anyway.

It's one thing to have professional drive. It's another to keep others from achieving their own destiny so you can cling to what you think is yours. What good does that do the world? Worse—what good does that do *you*? Believe me, if you're preventing upward mobility, everyone sees it and everybody knows why!

PIT STOP!

Personal Ramp: Transformative leaders are made not born. That's why they are called transformative—because they've transformed. What awareness of your good, bad, or ugly personal issues do you need to break through to become a transformative leader? What do you need to acknowledge that's not perfect in your life so that you can bring the reality of who you are to work?

____

____

____

____

____

Professional Ramp: How do you help team members become stronger, wiser, and better people? Are there any team members struggling with their own personal issues? Can you identify the things holding them back? How can you help them be better, stronger, and more confident?

____

____

____

____

____

If you look at great leaders throughout history, those who raised up the people around them went further faster and made a more lasting impact than those leaders who ruled with an iron fist. Whether you like it or not: Rule with jealously today and your statue will be toppled tomorrow. But rule with benevolence, care, and compassion and your work will carry on through the ages.

DESCRIBE YOUR PERSONAL BEST

When I was head of recruiting for HBO, there's a question I'd often ask out of the blue to colleagues, team members, and during my interviews with candidates. I'd simply ask them to describe for me how they show up as their best selves whether at school, at work, at home, at life. Not what *I think* their best should be, but what *they* personally think of as their best. In interviews, people are often thrown off by this question, either because they think most interviews are just an assessment of technical skills and basic personality or because they feel that there's some "right answer" that they have to hit for me to be impressed. But that's not what I'm doing. I truly want to know WHO you are and if YOU know who you are. I'm simply asking, "When you are at your best, what are you doing? What does it look like? How do you feel?"

When a woman came to tears after I asked her these questions, I think there were two reasons: first, no one had ever asked her before, and second, underneath those questions is the need to get connected—to merge your "work self" with your "true self" and make an assessment. Well, I asked her what the tears were about, and she said just that: "I feel like you are really trying to *see* me, and I'm not used to people caring that much." Many people haven't stopped to think about what they look like when they're running at top capacity; they're just coming in, doing their job, collecting their paycheck, and growing older. That's not enough.

When we ask people what their best looks like—and truly care about the answer—we show them we care about them as a human being, both inside and beyond the confines of this particular position. It's actually very powerful. And when they are finally ready and able to describe what it looks like when they are at their best—what they're doing, what they feel like—and are able to share it with you, that is a freeing moment for them, and also for you.

THERE'S NO EMMY AWARD FOR LEADERSHIP. THERE'S NO OSCAR. THE ONLY GLORY I CAN ACKNOWLEDGE IS THE PLEASURE OF SEEING THE PEOPLE AROUND ME REACHING THEIR HIGHEST POTENTIAL.

When my team members or applicants describe what their best looks like to me, I respond with, "That's also what I want for you. Let's make a plan to get you there. You're on my team—it's not about just doing what I want you to, or what you think you're supposed to do; it's about determining what your best is and reaching for it with all your might." I want my team members standing in the spotlight, humming with the full power of their best selves and realizing their fullest potential. I want them to deliver on the promise of the gifts that they have been given. That's what I'm here for as their leader. Leadership is service. It's not about me.

There's no Emmy Award for leadership. There's no Oscar. The only glory I can acknowledge is the pleasure of seeing the people around me reaching their highest potential. When people are doing their best, they're doing what's best for the company *and* what's best for themselves.

PIT STOP!

Personal Ramp: Describe a moment in your life where everything was running perfectly at top speed. What about this experience is important? How does this experience mirror your values? Get yourself in the mindset of when you were winning. What about this moment can you use and draw from to move forward?

____

____

____

____

Professional Ramp: What values did you see in the moment you described above? What values are important to you? Create a plan to incorporate these values into your professional life and think about how these values can lead to success in the workplace.

____

____

____

____

When leaders change, teams change. When teams change, businesses change. And when businesses change, the world they operate in changes. It's not about you being the star; it's about creating an environment that's conducive for people to bring in their best ideas, their best selves, and to shine.

At the end of the day, filling your floor with the best, brightest, sleekest, fastest, and most awe-inspiring speed machines known to the world is what's going to bring you the kind of attention that actually has any traction. True glory comes from an abundance of riches, not a scarcity. When you're ripping down the highway with your fantastic coterie of speed machines, it will be clear that no one but an enlightened leader could have put that crew in place.

LANE 5

"ALL ARE CONNECTED ... NO ONE THING CAN CHANGE BY ITSELF."

—PAUL HAWKEN

CHECK THE MAP

When Rome was expanding its power across the globe, one of the most important things the Romans built were roads. Why? The ability to connect people—to move from point A to point B and to make that connection smooth and easy to navigate—is paramount to civilization's forward movement.

Once the roads were in place, people needed maps that would show them how the roads connected. There is a certain power in maps, which comes from their ability to show us how to move, how to connect. They give us choices. They show us which ways are fast and which ways are beautiful. Which ways are lonely and which ways are densely populated with roadside attractions.

But I think a map's true power comes from this: even the smallest footpath in the most distant corner of the world is connected to where you are sitting or standing right this very second. Through time and space and human achievement, there is a way to go from anywhere in the world to anywhere else. And what shows us how to get there? Maps. All roads—and thereby, all humans—are connected through this vast web of interlocking lines and lives.

PUTTING YOURSELF IN THE PATH OF POSSIBILITY

This notion of "all roads lead to Rome" is truly about connections, namely, connections between people. It's up to us to choose whether or not we acknowledge these connections and whether we see them as opportunities to grow—to be greater, to do greater things.

As a little girl tracing the outlines of the photo of the Coliseum in the World Book Encyclopedia, I had no idea I was putting a pin in the signs that would one day lead me to the very steps up to the entrance to the Coliseum itself and the convergence of all the things I wanted in life coming true. That formative experience—the traveling encyclopedia salesman, my mother's intuition, my own curiosity—all worked together to start a road that would lead to Rome.

This feeling of connectivity first hit me over the head when I was fresh out of college, working at a JC Penney call center in Nashville. As the summer was coming to an end, I learned that Sprint was looking for long-distance operators. That was for me! I had just worked in a call center, so it was the perfect step up! I applied, got the job, and started that fall.

That job with Sprint actually began my communications career. I started out at $15/hour, the most money I'd ever made—and not a bad wage back then. I spent five years at Sprint, starting out on the call-center floor along with hundreds of other customer service reps. Even then, I knew my job on the floor was simply a stepping-stone. I needed more. I have always had this drive, this desire to achieve—and I knew there was opportunity for me to be better, learn more, give more, and do more.

I wanted to get out of that 24/7 call-center environment where work hours and schedules were dependent on tenure, and hundreds of people were slugging away at the same job. Within the second year, a position came open: front desk receptionist. I applied.

Out of all the other people who wanted to get out of that pool, I believe I won that promotion because I saw it as bigger than the way it was presented on the job description. Even at twenty-two, I knew that the only way I could move up was to put myself in a place where things happened. I wanted to *put myself in the path of possibility.* And certainly more things were happening at the front door than in the pit.

During my interview, I remember saying, "Yes, this is a front desk receptionist role, but here's how I can help you more. Not only am I answering phones and serving customers when they come in, I'm also sitting here next to the HR department. I can help them with the daily flurry of CSR applications by managing and organizing the process. I can even help with the candidate screening process since I know the job and know what it takes to be successful. I can schedule manager interviews and build interview loops for the supervisors. I can certainly do a lot more than answer phones." I sold the idea and got the job.

Putting myself in the pathway of possibility was dead on. I actually made a connection with the general manager of the building, who ended up giving me a piece of advice that changed the trajectory of my career. She was a powerful but approachable woman, and she saw my drive, determination, and willingness to grow and be more. She reached out to me and said, "Carla, I'm going to tell you something I wish someone had told me a long time ago: You will increase your odds of success as a woman in business if you stay mobile. In order to keep your career growing, it may mean moving to different locations and cities. Keep your life nimble. Just know that the path to success is easier for women when we're able to take advantage of opportunities that may not be just right down the street."

THERE WASN'T NECESSARILY A DESIRE AT THE HEART OF THAT RELOCATION; IT WAS MORE OF A SUMMONS. I JUST KNEW I HAD TO DO THIS

That advice has stayed with me and helped shape my career decisions ever since. It's why I'm in New York now; it's why I've lived in six different cities, many places where I had no friends or relatives. Just opportunity. And I doubt I would have received this advice on the call-center floor, where people often stayed planted awhile. Now certainly the "stay nimble" logic may not be as meaningful given today's technology advancements and virtual work environments. Back then, keeping my life simple and easy to relocate played a big part of my upward mobility.

As I settled in my new receptionist role, I began to grow both in knowledge and in my levels of duties, making the most of my little toehold in the world of promotion. After I'd been in my position about two years, one day the HR manager came back from a trip to headquarters in Kansas and stopped at my desk. She looked at me and said, "Carla, those Greek sorority letters on your mousepad are identical to the ones I saw on the desk of a woman I have been working with at corporate for the last few years. I should get you two connected."

I saw the opportunity and reached out. Through that connection with my sorority sister, I learned of an entry level position in the training deptartment at corporate. I applied, nailed the interview, and soon my car was packed, and I was driving across seven states to my new life.

There wasn't necessarily a *desire* at the heart of that relocation; it was more of a *summons*. I just knew I *had* to do this. And the fact I was on a road that connected me to where I was going—via my sorority sister—was so clear, so obvious, I just had to get on it and see where it would take me.

When I pulled into Kansas City with all my worldly possessions piled on the backseat of my car, my sorority sister had already found me an apartment, a parking space, and a safe place to land among people who cared about me and where I was going. She was lifting while climbing—as well as connecting.

That move led me to experiences, relationships, and scenarios that were to be some of the most endearing and toughest times in my life. After nearly twenty-five years, I can look back down that road and count the women (and men) who reached out to guide me and show me the way to the next connection. They are still part of my life today. I provided the get-up-and-go, but they were the ones who shined the light on the pathway and whispered, "Keep going … turn here … stop and refuel here."

PIT STOP!

Personal Ramp: Have you ever bypassed an opportunity or relationship because it looked challenging? Did you bypass because you didn't know how to read the map? Or did you not *want* to read it?

Professional Ramp: Do you see any opportunities where you might shape what you've assumed was a dead end into a path of possibility? Even a lateral move can sometimes be what's best for you to transform in the long run.

UNEXPECTED CONNECTIONS

I stayed in Kansas City two years, and knew it was time to make another move. A big one. All signs pointed toward Atlanta, Georgia—a virtual Mecca if you were young, black, upwardly mobile, and seeking to make something of yourself in corporate America in the 90's. That was definitely what I wanted for myself. I knew I had leadership capabilities—and the only way to lead was to take a leap.

Even though I was salaried when I was a coordinator at Sprint corporate, I took an hourly role to get to Atlanta, which was technically a step down. However, the move soon landed me in my first managerial position. Within a year of arriving, I left Sprint and was running a cable call center, putting my own ideas on the line, building operations from a 9-5 call center with only twenty-five customer-service representatives to a 24/7 center with a hundred reps. Next, I was developing new-hire and sales-training curriculum and delivering those courses in thirty-five small and large cities in Georgia, driving more effective customer service and increased sales by CSRs.

After a couple years through that call center manager job , I formed a relationship with our HBO rep. When she stepped down to relocate and build a family, she encouraged me to apply for her job. I did, and launched myself into the arms of HBO. All these roads were connecting on the map of my career, leading me to where I was meant to be, wanted to be.

All roads are connected, but it's up to each of us to *choose* to see those connections and to move on them. Work is often a place where those connections are sorely underrecognized—and underutilized. Many people miss opportunities because they don't recognize there even *was* an opportunity, or because it had some sort of inconvenience attached to it—extra work or a perceived step down before a big jump up. But with some strategic maneuvering, those paths often lead to big opportunities down the road.

When leaders create an environment of connectivity in the workplace, and promote a feeling of togetherness, they build an understanding that no matter how each employee or department chooses to get there, *there* is a unified destination. In essence, all roads in your company or on your team should be leading to some proverbial Rome—whether it's a financial goal, an expansion or acquisition, or simply a healthier work environment that promotes employee loyalty and longevity. The tricky part is mapping the route to your final (and ever changing) destination and making sure everyone is moving toward it.

You have to learn to inspire and empower your team members to make decisions and follow the right maps on their career paths. They will even delight you by finding pathways you've never even considered! As they choose their own paths, make sure they understand they're accountable for their decisions and actions. Freedom comes with responsibility and accountability. Be dedicated to their success and forward motion, but they still have a job to do and there's still a common destination. If they take too many detours or go the wrong way entirely, it's your job to help them get back on track.

One thing I'm known for is having people on my teams who end up being promoted quickly and moving successfully throughout the company. I believe I'm a catalyst for their movement: I help them find out what ignites them, what connects them to their work and to their coworkers, and I help clear the way. I try to do for them what my one of my high school teachers (and others) did for me: see more in me than I saw in myself.

To do that, I start by finding out what inspires my team members. If you can figure out how to incorporate your team's passions into their work life, you're already halfway there. While they still have to put in the work and provide the get-up-and-go, I try to find a way to give them a softer landing at their destination, just like my sorority sister did for me back in Kansas City. And, just like my HR manager back at Sprint in Nashville, just like my HBO leaders and believers did for me. I have my eyes and ears open, helping them to discover the hidden connections that are already on the map, so they can move courageously from Point A to Point B.

This has yet to backfire on me. Putting my team members on the pathway of possibility and teaching them how to seek it for themselves has always engendered a sense of togetherness and loyalty. After all, if all roads are connected—and I truly believe they are—there's a very high chance that you'll run into them again ... Hopefully, they'll remember you as a proactive and encouraging person in their lives and will extend goodwill, and maybe even work to return the favor by sending someone wonderful your way. What goes around comes around—so make sure what you're sending out is worth catching again someday. You never know how connections will play out down the road.

PUTTING MY TEAM MEMBERS ON THE PATHWAY OF POSSIBILITY AND TEACHING THEM HOW TO SEEK IT FOR THEMSELVES HAS ALWAYS ENGENDERED A SENSE OF TOGETHERNESS AND LOYALTY.

PIT STOP!

Personal Ramp: What people in your personal life can you connect to help other people?

____

____

____

____

____

____

Professional Ramp: What's a current or past professional connection that helped get you where you are today? What's a connection that can help get you where you want to go? How can you use that connection to help your team?

____

____

____

____

____

____

LEADERSHIP FROM EVERY SEAT

This idea of creating an environment of connectivity is something I've been saying to my team for the past twenty years as a leader. My role is to create an environment that's conducive to making people want to bring their best ideas to work. Now, if I believe that, then I have to create space for them to share those ideas.

I've mentioned this all before, but I think it bears repeating: Leadership is not just for leaders. I believe in leadership from every seat. Wherever you sit, whatever part of the business and part of the work you touch, you too have an opportunity to contribute and add value. You, too, may have thoughts and ideas around your very own work. Why would I not create a space for people to do that?

The reason why I'm so transparent about what I'm working on is I know I can't fully carry or achieve goals and objectives without their input. I show my team I am vulnerable, even in my strength, even when I come across as being powerful and in charge. People say, "Oh my gosh, you probably run everything by just showing up." I say, "Actually, I am just as vulnerable as I am strong." If there's something I know, I'll tell you. If there's something I don't know, I tell you that too. That builds trust.

Being trustworthy allows people to offer up ideas without risk. Vulnerability is key. You build connectivity when they see the environment is safe. They think, *I trust that I can say this, or raise my hand, or have commentary, or bring something to the table without punishment, jealousy, criticism, or retribution.*

In one of my roles at HBO, I had a team member request a meeting to present an idea. "Carla, for two weeks I've been trying to present this idea to you. I had to get myself together. I knew I had to come with my proposal buttoned up as best as I can. Here's the idea I have …"

Let me tell you, it was a bombshell of a proposal. She had an idea I had never even thought of. I said, "This idea hasn't even crossed my mind. Just imagine if you kept this to yourself. The company would not have benefitted at all! Now, let's talk about how to advance your plan."

She said, "I know for a fact I would have never done this if you hadn't forced us to think critically," Then she said, "I wouldn't have thought of it either, if it wasn't for the new way we do things here."

You may have noticed use of the word "forced." At the beginning, people are often resistant to doing more and being more. At the beginning, my team members come to me and say, "Carla, I'm uncomfortable thinking like this. I'm uncomfortable being free to roam and being accountable. I don't want to get in trouble." We've been trained to be fearful of accountability. That has to stop.

I let my team members know that accountability would certainly be tied to what they did. They'd have to get used to that idea, even if it made them uncomfortable. *Get comfortable with the uncomfortable.* Nothing changes if it always feels easy. Unless we shift to a place where people are feeling out of sorts a bit, we won't enact any great change. From change springs growth.

> **THE SAD FACT IS THAT MOST PEOPLE ARE NEVER ASKED TO TRULY CONTRIBUTE IN THEIR LIVES, NOT BY THEIR PARENTS, NOT BY THEIR TEACHERS. THEY JUST GET PULLED ALONG BEHIND THE CART.**

The sad fact is that most people are never asked to truly contribute in their lives, not by their parents, not by their teachers. They just get pulled along behind the cart. However, civilization thrives on innovation, and innovation only comes from fearless exploration.

Growth, development, expansion, and discovery are essential. Every day I entertain the notion there's someone right there in front of me with something inside him or her that only has to be given the space to emerge in order to change the world. I like to see people that way, I think, in part, because that's how I would like people to see me—and how I would like to see myself.

PIT STOP!

Personal Ramp: How can you help someone closest to you choose the more challenging but rewarding path?

____

____

____

____

____

____

Professional Ramp: How can you be the fork in a co-workers path to help them grow positively?

____

____

____

____

____

____

LEAD CHANGES: NAVIGATING OUTSIDE YOUR COMFORT ZONE

When I took the head of recruiting role at HBO, I was far outside my comfort zone. I didn't come from an HR background—but there was something over the mountain and I just had to go see! Yes, it was risky, but I jumped in with both feet; and I wanted my new team to come with me. At the first team huddle, I said, "Guys, let's re-imagine, re-engineer, and re-innovate this department. How talent acquisition looks today could be something different, not just because of me but because of you." Of course, they were all looking at me like, who is this woman? But bit by bit, change came.

I humbled myself and was as open as possible, telling the team, "You are the talent acquisition and recruiting experts. I just got here. I'm absolutely going to need you. We will carve a path forward together. In this new space, we're moving in a new direction. I need all of you to make change happen."

And with that, I opened the door for them to share ideas for improvement many had been wanting to share or kept close to their chests. I encouraged them to talk to one another—to talk to me. More than that, to be the experts and grow their knowledge and build their craft.

During that first huddle, my new team members were very quiet, and the first person who came to me after the meeting said, "Carla, I just want you to know we're so happy you're here. Everyone is blown away. If you noticed, the room was really quiet. We don't know if you're for real."

I said, "Thank you for sharing that with me. I promise you won't have to figure out if it's for real or not. There's a saying in the South,

'Don't talk about it. *Be* about it.' I'm getting ready to show you what I'm about and show you I'm real. I want you guys to do the same."

Unfortunately, many corporate cultures don't always breed humble leaders who see their team members as anything other than children to be managed. I choose to see people as we were all created—vibrant beings, each with talents and purpose, who can come together to do anything we put our minds to, as long as we're honest and brave. I was lucky to have been able to move so freely in a new role in a new department, because my senior leadership trusted my vision and my expertise to carry it out.

You may drop this news on your team and immediately people respond with creativity and renewed energy—or, more likely, you'll find that some people are resistant to the change, even fearful. That's okay too. You need to be prepared for human nature to come rushing at you, especially when you change fifteen, twenty, thirty people's lives all at once. That's a life tsunami. When you push your arm out into the ocean that hard, sometimes a big old wave comes rushing back. Stand firm, stay on message, and you will not only survive it, you'll wash away the debris that was there before.

PIT STOP!

Personal Ramp: What's a gift that's gathering dust, that you could brush off and share with others?

____

____

____

____

Professional Ramp: What will you do this week to discover the hidden talents of your team members?

____

____

____

____

ENLIGHTENED LEADERS GIVE AWAY THE SPOTLIGHT

If you are an enlightened leader, you should be able to apply those skills to any department, as long as the people in that department know their business. You are not there to be an expert in X, Y, and Z. You are there to lead a team of experts in X, Y, and Z to even greater success and innovation.

If the word "enlightened" gives you a queasy stomach, just substitute the word "exceptional." *Exceptional leadership.* The reason I like the word "enlightened," though, is because the word itself speaks to a lessening of burdens and a shining of light. There's something beautiful about that. When you use these practices with your team, you're taking a lot of the pressure off yourself as a leader and properly distributing responsibility. You're asking people to be talented, thinking adults headed toward a common goal, not sulky children shepherded toward your vision.

YOU ARE NOT THERE TO BE AN EXPERT IN X, Y, AND Z. YOU ARE THERE TO LEAD A TEAM OF EXPERTS IN X, Y, AND Z TO EVEN GREATER SUCCESS AND INNOVATION.

As you become enlightened in your leadership, it's important to share those changes with those around you. You want your team members inspired and prepared to make their own decisions so you can start using them as resources to draw upon. Once people start to understand you expect them to bring their *whole selves* to the table, you might be surprised what connections they make (and what inventive solutions and tactics they come up with).

It's making sure that James in accounting, who has a gift of writing or drawing or imagery, has a space and a reason to deliver on the promise of that gift at work or in life. It's making sure that Susan in sales, who has a gift of organizing groups and making people feel noticed, has a way to incorporate that gift into her success at the office. When team members begin to see each other as whole people with talents and interests beyond their job, it creates a sense of reality and connectivity. You become the fork in somebody else's road. They become more fulfilled individually, their bonds with leaders and coworkers deepen, and their sense of loyalty is increased. They know you don't just see them as Employee #5541. You see them as a whole person.

Again, leadership it not just for leaders. Whatever part of the business they're in or whatever part of the work they touch, all employees have an opportunity to significantly contribute and add value to the common good of the company. They may have thoughts and ideas around their work that could crack something open for the entire team or even the entire company. We have to create a space where people feel safe to do that and put a team win ahead of our own personal scorecard.

LANE 6

"EVEN THE RISK OF FAILING IS MORE APPEALING THAN STAYING THE SAME."

—CARLA MOORE

GO OFF-ROAD

Typically, going off-road means you start driving somewhere even when you don't know what the road looks like. I've gone off-road many times, and each time it's brought me to a new level of personal growth and development. It was a big jump to go from Centerville to Murfreesboro to Kansas City. (Finally! I lived in a place most Americans could find on a map.) But perhaps the biggest move I've made was leaving the comfort of nearly eleven years in Chicago and going off-road to HBO in New York where there were more people in the building than in my hometown.

NEW PATHS, NEW DESTINATIONS

If Atlanta was the Mecca for the young, black, upwardly mobile corporate set, then Chicago was like Oz. There was something magical about the Windy City that pulled many of the best and brightest west.

Within two years of landing in Atlanta, and while at HBO, I asked for a Chicago bid. They sent me north … to Minneapolis. Now, Minneapolis is a lovely city and people are very nice there, but it's bone-numbing cold and, from what I could tell, there wasn't a lot of diversity. I needed more cultural diversity to truly feel at home.

Not long after arriving in Minnesota, I literally raised my hand and asked again to be moved to Chicago. I knew I had more to give. Six months after arriving in Minneapolis, they sent me directly to the Windy City. For the second time in six months, I picked up and moved again, with no map, no marked trail. My client accounts got bigger, my territories grew and grew, and the impact I could make grew exponentially too. I was putting myself in the pathway of possibility once again. That's something that off-roading especially tends to do.

In Chicago, I hunkered down for over a decade. It's where I built my leadership career at HBO. I was taking on the largest accounts I'd seen up to that point, and in my fourth year there, I was promoted to Senior Sales Development Executive. I was making friends, making my mark, traveling a lot … and I was physically at my heaviest—nearly 350 pounds. That meant every time I traveled, I had to ask the flight attendant for a seatbelt extension, just so I could buckle up. To top it off, I'd just blasted through a three-month marriage that had drained me emotionally and spiritually.

I realized I needed something positive to counterbalance the poor decisions I'd made with my health and love life. I wanted more credibility, more training. I wanted to take myself and my journey more seriously. It was time to take bold steps, so I walked into Keller Graduate School and said, "I'd like to see what your school is like." That day, I enrolled in a full MBA program, taking classes at night while I held down my corporate job during the day. I was still traveling most of the week, going through a quickie divorce, finding a new place to live, and working part-time in my friend's hair salon on weekends. And since that didn't seem to be enough change, I decided I'd lose 100 pounds before walking across the stage to accept my MBA.

In that most difficult year, I realized the old maps weren't working for me any longer. I took a deep breath and walked out into the darkness, knowing that no matter where I went, each step was taking me further away from where I'd been.

IN THAT MOST DIFFICULT YEAR, I REALIZED THE OLD MAPS WEREN'T WORKING FOR ME ANY LONGER. I TOOK A DEEP BREATH AND WALKED OUT INTO THE DARKNESS, KNOWING THAT NO MATTER WHERE I WENT, EACH STEP WAS TAKING ME FURTHER AWAY FROM WHERE I'D BEEN.

PIT STOP!

Personal Ramp: If you knew that making a change would create the life you've always imagined, how would you do it? This isn't about looking at pros and cons, this is about the one big win you could achieve by going off-road.

____

____

____

____

____

Professional Ramp: Are you willing to go off-road to take a professional risk? What's your story of leadership transformation that you share with others?

____

____

____

____

____

FIND A WAY OR MAKE ONE

Nothing is more exciting than deciding for yourself which way you will go and forging ahead on an unknown course. In the movies, when the going gets tough, the movie stars seem to "get going" through vast, thick jungles, chopping their way through with a machete. Even if it's hard, they never stop, as if they know the sacred ruby is just on the other side of those vines … then—*VOILA!*—suddenly they've made it to the clearing and there's the treasure, just waiting for them to leap over the pits of snakes to claim it.

Life isn't really that different from the movies. During that difficult year in Chicago, I was cutting my way through the vines, trusting that someday, if I just didn't stop, I'd finally break through into the clearing and reap my reward. I heard someone say once, "Good things take time, but great things happen all at once." Often, that unflappable "movie-hero" approach is exactly the attitude we need to take in our own lives. An adventure movie is no good if the hero gives up—and who are you other than the hero of the greatest adventure of your life?

The most heightened moments in life begin as we leave the boundaries of our comfort zones. Moving into a place where the rules are unknown, being unsure and having to make your way—these are the situations that breed innovation and discovery in our lives.

One of the most insidious fears many people have is the fear of moving forward. This may manifest as an aversion to success or masquerade as a penchant for all things known and comfortable. The desire to dig in your heels and stick to the status quo may stem from a fear of failure or what people may think. It may come from knowing that once you push beyond the day-to-day, nothing will ever be the same again. Deep down, most people are terrified of change. The only problem with that is, you'll never go somewhere new—or be someone new—if you don't change what you're doing.

In Lane 2, we spoke about the difference between movement and remaining static: progress vs. perfection. When you take a big leap forward, you are embracing movement—embracing progress—in its most elemental form. You *become* the change. You live it and breathe it as it reverberates out from you, touching everyone and everything in your path.

THE MOST HEIGHTENED MOMENTS IN LIFE BEGIN AS WE LEAVE THE BOUNDARIES OF OUR COMFORT ZONES. MOVING INTO A PLACE WHERE THE RULES ARE UNKNOWN, BEING UNSURE AND HAVING TO MAKE YOUR WAY—THESE ARE THE SITUATIONS THAT BREED INNOVATION AND DISCOVERY IN OUR LIVES.

Change can be scary, but it's vital to our survival on this planet. There's a buzz-phrase that's been out there for some time now, "Adapt or die." Look around and you'll see that it's true. The businesses (and people!) that last the longest are the most able to shift, grow, and adapt to change.

You don't have to do huge things to make a big difference. If change is difficult for you, start by doing simple things: Walk or drive a new way to work. Change your routine by moving your desk or your bed. Flip your weekend schedule on its head. Little changes, one after another, become a pattern, then a habit, then a new way of life. And once you get used to the little changes and the unexpected—and often welcome—surprises they bring, you'll be ready to introduce bigger, more significant changes into your life.

Keep in mind, though, that when you're really ready for truly sustainable change, you need to be prepared to go off road. There is no easy way through the jungle. There were many times I quit, full stop, on my journey. Frankly, I was too soft on myself. *You deserve a break,* I say to myself. *You deserve a donut. You deserve to have what you want right now.* Once I stopped being so soft on myself and so soft on goal achievement, that's when things started to snap into place. If you have a destination or a goal for your life, you literally *have to* get it done. You cannot put it off forever, because forever is something that is granted to no one. You *must* find a way to apply yourself to your dream today and every day.

Here's an example. I didn't know *how* I was going to study and attend night classes when I was on the road so much, but I found a way to break my trips up so I could come back to Chicago to take a class, then fly out to go hit the next two cities on my agenda, and send my homework in while I was on the road. If you truly want something, you will find ways to make it happen!

In addition, my night classes after work lasted three hours, and because I was dedicated to my weight-loss regimen, I made sure to pack the right things for dinner and snack. The only problem was that the school's student break room had a refrigerator but no microwave for my Lean Cuisine dinners. At first, I actually started taking up a collection from other students to buy a microwave—halfway through, I realized as a salesperson the answer is always "no"—unless you ask.

So I headed to management. I knew I needed to put myself in position to win, so I thought beyond the limitation, and when I told the school I was going to buy a microwave, to their great credit, they said "no, we'll put one in every break room." And those microwaves are still in each Chicago location today. If going off-road seems intimidating, consider the rewards along the way make it worth it.

When I finally walked across the stage to receive the diploma for my MBA in 2002, I was nearly eighty-five pounds lighter than when I'd started, thanks in part to those microwave Lean Cuisine meals.

I want you to be constantly prepared to forge ahead on unknown courses. There's nothing more exhilarating than going off-road. Now, exhilarating doesn't always mean fun—a roller coaster is exhilarating, but there are times you think you might be scared out of your mind coming down that hill—but it does light a sense of *aliveness* in you, a level of presence that ignites your passion and drives everything you do.

Me walking across the stage isn't the end of the story, because at that point I stopped dieting and the weight began to climb back up again. What I missed in my transformation to lose weight and gain an MBA was the mental-emotional piece. I learned years later that physical transformation requires engagement of all other senses, aspects, and functions of who you are—spiritual, emotional, mental. I only had the physical in place, so there was no way it was going to stick.

It's the same when it comes to the benefits of off-roading. You can go down a path you've never gone down before, but unless you're also taking notes and watching and learning as you go, you're going to have to drive through that same patch of jungle all over again. You can't just go kamikaze. What good will that do you? Unfortunately, I didn't know that then. I went down the same road a few more times. It wasn't until my big crash moment when I truly saw the light.

PIT STOP!

Personal Ramp: What's an off-road-type thing (earning your MBA; asking for a microwave) that you need to add to your own life? What could that one act mean to others? What's the reward?

____

____

____

____

Professional Ramp: When was the last time you went off-road in your role or career? What did that look like? What insight or reward did you get from that experience? If you were to go off-road again today, what would it look like? What could it mean for others?

____

____

____

____

EDUCATE YOUR TRAVEL PARTNERS

While you may have your understanding finally in place, be mindful that even though you're ready to leap, others may not be. This is true for your friends, family, and team members, but it's also true for your fellow colleagues in leadership. When they see you making big changes, they may decide they don't like you rocking the boat.

Change is scary, remember? And that includes change tangentially forced upon you by an enlightened coworker or friend. There is a big difference between ignorance and understanding, and the only thing that leads from the first to the second is education.

DO YOUR BEST TO EXPLAIN WHY EMBRACING THESE CHANGES AND TAKING THESE RISKS IS GOING TO BE POSITIVE OVERALL. DON'T BE AFRAID TO SHARE WITH OTHERS ABOUT WHAT YOU SEE. HELP THEM SEE YOUR VISION FOR THE WAY THINGS COULD BE.

With your team members and colleagues, be prepared to do some encouraging, but don't tarry. Leap when you know it's time to leap, and set the bar high. At the same time, do your best to explain why embracing these changes and taking these risks is going to be positive overall. Don't be afraid to share with others about what you see. Help them see your vision for the way things could be.

Share your own personal experiences and get ready to hold a hand or two, at least at first, as people get used to what you're doing. Be sure of what you know and honest about what you don't know. As you become more fearless—as more of your off-road adventures prove to be fruitful over time—the more likely people will take chances with you, even when some of the ideas don't work out.

PIT STOP!

Personal Ramp: What conversation do you need to have with family or friends to help them see how you're taking positive risks?

____

____

____

____

____

Professional Ramp: For coworkers resistant to change, what could you say to them to help them see why you're embracing change?

____

____

____

____

____

RISKS SHOW WHO YOU ARE

Leadership isn't only about getting everyone else where they need to go. You need to be in a place where you, *yourself*, can make a significant impact!

When I went through that crazy year and came through it—finally finishing night school, walking across that stage MBA in hand, weighing eighty-five pounds less, divorce done, getting ready to move to a new apartment, promoted at work—it seemed insane, so much had taken place so quickly. My approach to work has never been the same since. To go through all of those life changes in such a compact amount of time and to come out on the other side, not only alive but thriving, gave me a feeling I could try anything that came my way, even if I was doubtful about the outcome. Risk-taking became easier, and that translated directly to my work.

After that year, I was much more present at work. I started showing up and placing myself in the path of possibility in a serious way—no more hiding in the shadows. Up to this point, I had taken the biggest risk at work by actually asking for a meeting with the highest-ranking executive on the team. I knew I was ready for a promotion, but there wasn't an opening … yet. I knew I would have to go for it and make known what I wanted and that I had the capacity to do more. It was time to go off-road again.

It was one of the riskiest moments in my career. I approached my boss's boss (with my direct boss's blessing of course) and set up the meeting, electing to meet at a cable conference where we would be able to do something informal for a few minutes between conference sessions. After we sat down and caught up a bit, I took my chance and said, "I see where you want to take this team and I share in that vision. I absolutely want to be a part of the future growth of this business and play a larger role on the team. I just finished my MBA, and I know I have much more to offer. I'm looking for ways now to maximize my contributions to this team, to our clients and to this company. I believe I'm ready for the responsibility of a position at the next level. I'm ready to step up and do the necessary things to help you move this team and our business forward."

Asking for what I wanted and letting my big boss know what I felt I had to offer was a risk, and she responded beautifully. In fact, she said, "Carla, the professional maturity you've shown by saying to me, 'This is who I am. This is what I know I can do and contribute,' is courageous and will not go unnoticed. I can't promise you anything sitting right here on this bench here in Boston, but I *can* say that now I know who you are."

Do we really know the passions, gifts, talents, hearts, and dreams of what people may need and want? Do other people know ours? No. Not unless we connect to them and *tell* them. This particular boss was from the New York office while I was in Chicago She didn't know me from a can of paint. But after that meeting, I was on her mind. When something new came up, she wondered, "Would this be a match for the woman I spoke to at the conference in Boston?" Six months after that meeting, I was promoted to account executive, then quickly promoted again to account manager. She would be one of the most instrumental factors of my career growth at HBO.

This risk-taking approach is one I've been teaching others since I began leading teams. If there is something you know you can do or that you need and want, remember that others won't know about it if it stays locked inside your head or your heart. As a leader, I won't know what's inside of you until you share it with me. There's a risk factor in this—but there's a great reward too. In opening yourself up and taking a risk, you become memorable; you cease being a can of paint. You become a living, breathing person in others' eyes.

To sell anything—including yourself—you have to craft a narrative that will compel someone to say, "You know what? I can see what you're talking about. I'm going to take a chance on you." You need to tie your heart, dreams, and ego to how your narrative is going to be meaningful to the business. It's not enough to know you're ready for it. Give your leader a business plan. Back it up with hard facts. Tell a story in numbers. Show where you can be of service and why you're worth more.

FUEL FOR THOUGHT

How are you memorable in your interactions? To be memorable, you've got to stand out. Know your story, know it pat, and be able to tell it in a compelling way. For example, what's your story of leadership transformation that you share with others?

Speaking of embracing risk, I say to people that my leadership actually got stronger when I stopped being afraid of getting fired. I learned that notion from one of my senior leaders at HBO. Without that fear I became more and more creative. See, most people "stay in the box" because its safe, and if my head is not poking out, I won't get shot. For me, releasing the fear of being fired was a fuelmaker. I knew I was good and committed to the work and the brand, so what was I afraid of? So I became bolder. I also started making a bigger impact, because my risks, ideas, and thoughts were broader and more far-reaching. When there is fear in an environment or within you, your thoughts are limited. Your creativity gets limited. Your risk-taking gets limited. When you create unlimited viewpoints that generates room for possibilities and creativity, you then open the room up to all types of solutions to problems.

This also means saying, "I'm an adult." You let go of that child-parent role. No one will take you seriously if you are always in a place of fear and subservience. I know that may not go over well with people, particularly during times of uncertainty—people are already nervous—but sometimes you have to take your leadership nearly to the point where you could get fired in the name of good business decision making. To get to the clearing on the other side of the jungle, you have to cut a path through the section that was off-limits just moments before.

PIT STOP!

Personal Ramp: What off-road risk can you take to unlock your potential?

____

____

____

____

____

Professional Ramp: How can you go off-road at work to show who you are?

____

____

____

____

____

LANE 7

"SOMETIMES IT IS NECESSARY TO SIT IN PEACE AND QUIET JUST SO YOU CAN HEAR YOURSELF THINK. SLOW IT DOWN. TAKE A BREATH. ESCAPE, SO YOU CAN FIND YOURSELF AGAIN. DRAW CLARITY AND STRENGTH FROM SERENITY AND CALM. CONNECT WITH YOURSELF. GROUND AND CENTER. ASK FOR GUIDANCE FROM THE DIVINE. SPEND TIME WITH YOUR SPIRITUALITY."

—AKIROQ BROST

SLOW DOWN TO POWER UP

I've often thought that constant motion looks an awful lot like running away. Sometimes, focusing on "what's next" leaves the rest of the world focused on your taillights.

Every now and again, you need to pull over, slow down, get out the map, and take a good look at what got you to where you are now. Very likely, the road that brought you to your current destination will not be the same road that takes you to your next destination. If you're not absolutely sure where you're headed and how you're going to get there, it's time to *stop, assess, strategize, and plan* your next move.

CRASH. BREATHE. DRIVE.

In the middle of that insane, intense time in Chicago when I was constantly off-road and going a million miles a minute both day and night, I crashed several times. It was inevitable. These weren't the *big* crashes that changed my life, but I had a series of warnings—situations where it seemed like the whole universe was trying to get me to stop, sit up, and take notice that this was my *life,* and I was simply racing through it. If I was to fulfill my own personal destiny, apparently the universe would have to send me bigger and bigger messages until I finally got the picture. My 90-day marriage was one of those messages.

My husband had been my boyfriend in Minneapolis, and he eventually followed me to Chicago. Being a good Southern girl and not wanting to live together, I married him. But what *really* sent me to the courthouse to marry a man I wasn't in love with? Why didn't I listen to my body, voice, and spirit when I was crying out the night before—knowing I didn't want to go through with it? Why didn't alarms go off as I put on a black dress instead of a white one? Every fiber of my being was trying to tell me to stop … why didn't I listen to myself? Why didn't I think I deserved to marry someone I actually *loved*?

There is a saying that you marry to the level of your self-esteem. I know it's true every time I look back and realize that I chose to bring a man into my life and to enter into a sacred union with him, against my better judgment. Three months later, I was sitting on my sofa, married and miserable, wondering how to get out of this awful situation.

There's another saying I like: "When the student is ready, the teacher appears." I'd been taught that my whole life. At that moment on my sofa on a day off in Chicago, I, like many people tuned in to an *Oprah* episode. She was featuring a new psychologist on her show who was promoting his book. His name was Dr. Phil, and the book was called *Self Matters: Creating Your Life From The Inside Out.* He began to say things I had just begun asking myself: *Why do I do what I do? Why do*

I make certain decisions? Why do I choose certain scenarios? He asked viewers to list the ten most defining moments of their lives, the seven most critical choices that put them on their current path, and the five most pivotal people in their world. The idea was that these things would give us insights into what shaped us, who shaped us, how we got on this current path, and how we could remold ourselves in order to live the life we wanted.

I picked up a pen, did the exercise, and hung it up above my desk on the corkboard. That was September 1999 and I still have those lists. Here's what they said:

10 Most Defining Moments

1. **Sudden death of my only brother**
2. **Parents divorce while I was in college**
3. **Getting baptized at church camp at fifteen**
4. **First boyfriend at fifteen (was not claimed publicly)**
5. **Attending college**
6. **First out of state move to Kansas City (where I knew no one)**
7. **Losing first 100 pounds (noticing different treatment)**
8. **Landing first formal leadership role (Atlanta)**
9. **Getting hired by HBO**
10. **Getting married (but not wanting to)**

7 Most Critical Choices

1. Finishing high school
2. Running for BETA club president
3. Getting my college degree
4. Getting my MBA
5. Learning another trade (opening a hair salon)
6. Marrying someone not in love with
7. Choosing divorce quickly

5 Most Pivotal People

1. My mother—for her teaching and guidance
2. My father—dating habits and ideas about men have certainly been shaped by him
3. Only brother—taught me about real life, truth teller, taught me how to drive, taught me how to read a map (literally)
4. My second-grade teacher, Miss Sullivan, for acknowledging how smart I was and making me feel valued
5. BFF (became fast friends as adults and has touched my life in every area)

Looking at those lists, I knew I had to get to the bottom of why I now weighed 350 pounds. I knew there had to be something more than just cheeseburgers, fried chicken, and caramel cake. There was something else I was carrying—something heavy—and the weight was the outward symptom. Doing Dr. Phil's exercise was the first time I started to get connected to the idea that there was something deeper at work, more than just the basic science that told me to eat less and move more.

When I looked at myself in the mirror, I looked completely the opposite from how I considered a successful person should look. I saw someone who had to work fifty times harder to be taken seriously, to prove she was smart and of value, to convince people she wasn't just overweight and lazy and out of control. For the first time, I started to see that the weight was the counterbalance to this insanely hectic life I was leading. I was constantly running, trying to prove I was worth knowing.

I KNEW THERE HAD TO BE SOMETHING MORE THAN JUST CHEESEBURGERS, FRIED CHICKEN, AND CARAMEL CAKE. THERE WAS SOMETHING ELSE I WAS CARRYING—SOMETHING HEAVY—AND THE WEIGHT WAS THE OUTWARD SYMPTOM.

What I didn't know, yet, was that my overachievement was a way of adding value to myself. Growing up, everyone else in my family was lighter-skinned, attractive, and fit; I was not. I always saw myself as "less than." I didn't realize then that I felt I had to add value to myself by being smarter, funnier, more helpful—by giving the best gifts; by being the best, most compassionate friend; by sacrificing myself for other's comfort ... by marrying someone I didn't love so he could have a place to live in Chicago.

Sitting there on the sofa that day, after completing Dr. Phil's exercise, was like the moment after a crash. You realize you're still alive, you're still breathing. Now it's time to get your car back on the road and drive away. For me, at that moment, this first meant taking the steps I needed to end my marriage.

WHAT I KNOW NOW IS WE ARE BORN WITH VALUE—SO MUCH VALUE THAT IT CAN'T BE ADDED TO. WE ARE VALUABLE UPON WAKING, WITH EVERY BREATH WE BREATHE.

I didn't know how to make the change stick, though. I didn't know how to do the work that would solve the *problem* instead of focusing on the *symptoms*. What I know now is we are born with value—so much value that it can't be added to. We are valuable upon waking, with every breath we breathe. Babies know this intrinsically; they reach out, demanding to be fed, to be loved, to be cared for. But sometimes, as we move through the world, we suffer damage that convinces us that our value is not inherent or infinite. Then, after suffering the blows of life, we must truly take the time to stop, reset, and refocus on why we are here and what we are doing.

Crash. Breathe. Drive on.

PIT STOP!

Personal Ramp: If you keep seeing the same mile markers over and over and you're not closer to your destination—these are signs that it's time to pull over. Ask yourself: How do I know I'm in the right place? What are the signs I'm becoming the person I want to be?

____

____

____

____

Professional Ramp: Do you have low energy in your roles? Is it hard to come in each day? Recharging is staying actively engaged, continuing to expand your network at work and in your industry. How can you recharge *at* work?

____

____

____

____

BRAKE TO BREAK FREE

Your plan for where you want to go and how you're going to get there is important. So it's essential that you stop every now and then to make sure you're still on course.

Take even thirty minutes out of your busy schedule on the weekend and pull off the mental highway of your life. Where are you? Are you where you expected to be? What's stopping you? Are you taking full control of your actions and decisions? Where are you in the lives of other people? Are you someone they can count on? Are you someone they turn to for help? Do they trust you? Who are your friends? Do they love you? How do you know? Who do you love? How do you know?

If you find this is difficult, don't be too hard on yourself ... but don't be too easy on yourself, either. You may not always have time to set aside so you can think critically. But the problem with not stopping to take a breath is that you'll only get more of the same. To break free, you might need to brake for a little bit.

THE PROBLEM WITH NOT STOPPING TO TAKE A BREATH IS THAT YOU'LL ONLY GET MORE OF THE SAME. TO BREAK FREE, YOU MIGHT NEED TO BRAKE FOR A LITTLE BIT.

No one else cares about your path the way you do. While the people around you may very well care for you and want the best for you, everyone has his or her own personal agenda. Only *you* know exactly what is best for you. It's time to affirm your place in the grand scheme of things and make sure where you are is where you really want to be. And once you get that clarity, it's with you for life. Enlightenment is irreversible.

PIT STOP!

Personal Ramp: Don't set the GPS and forget it. Calculate your own route--there's the quick route, the scenic route, and then the best route for you. You have a destination in mind, but how could you take a different path?

____

____

____

____

Professional Ramp: This week, explore opportunities to support another department, ancillary to your business. What could be those opportunities?

____

____

____

____

MY 3P EQUATION

During my speaking events, I talk a lot about my 3P Equation—Passion + Purpose = Power. *Passion* is what drives you. It creates wild emotion, energy, and excitement in your life. You can have many passions. Passion is for *you*—but *purpose* is for others. Purpose is often clear and singular. It is how you serve the world. It gives your life meaning, direction, and focus. *Power* is what happens when you bring passion and purpose together. You need all three.

Since 2007, I've lived with these three Ps as my guide, and I am happy to share them everywhere I go. These are three key components of how personal enlightenment transformed my life and maximized my potential at home and at work. I can only imagine if I had been told this when I was at the start of my career, or when I was a kid, how much sooner I could have achieved happiness and success and could share it to help others.

You see, many people think success is all about the school you attend, the degrees you have, the internship programs you complete and the size of your power network. While all this is important, and you can get pretty far with those things, I believe my 3P equation can help maximize your contributions to everything you're a part of.

PASSION

Life is nothing without passion.

We've all heard the saying "follow your passion." Sounds cliché but its true. Passion is what fuels you. It's what starts the engine. Passion is the energy that keeps you going, that keeps you filled with meaning and excitement and anticipation. Passion helps you accomplish anything you set your mind to and enables you to experience life at home and at work to the utmost.

To find your passion, you must spend time thinking about, connecting with, and exploring your heart's true desires. Ask yourself what do you wish for? What do you want? What's important to you about that? If you got it, what would be different? You have to get back to what you love, if you're not there already. And if you're not, then step one is to start a "Passion List." Write down everything you like. What really excites you inside? What parts of your current role at work would you actually do for free? What are you doing when time just flies by … at work or in life?

It's imperative that you be honest! You may be most passionate about your work, your children, football, or gardening. You may be passionate about the arts, cars, or fitness. Whatever it is that gets you going, own it! It may take a little while to come to the answers—in some cases weeks or months—but dedicate time to discovering what you're passionate about. That clarity will pay you dividends for life.

Unfortunately, I didn't spend time doing this when I was a young professional—even up until my "crash moment". I was not clear on the front end of my professional career about what I wanted. And what ended up happening was a ten-year career that was steady but not particularly meaningful.

I got caught up in the corporate rat race—an endless, self-defeating, mindless pursuit of promotions. I forgot to live mindfully. I was only thinking ahead, about where I was going next, forgetting to celebrate where I had come from.

As leaders, we must stop sometimes and stand in a space of gratitude to show appreciation for what we've already received. If not, you'll start to feel inadequate, because maybe you're not moving as fast as someone you were hired with or as fast as some timeline you had to hit.

As I got clearer and began to transform personally (not just physically but mentally, emotionally, spiritually), I noticed the positive impact it had on my leadership at work. I began to lead from a place of peace and authenticity, no longer feeling a need to compete and prove.

I began to carry a humble confidence in knowing who I am, what I am here to do, and what I'm in it for. For a long time, I knew I had a passion for teaching and helping others succeed, but I never truly owned it as a passion, which kept me unsure. Today I am passionate about personal power and enlightened leadership. That's my thing.

And as I began to grow and expand, my team also began to grow and expand. They were happy and getting promoted quicker. So HBO gave me more and more people. My sales territories began to grow exponentially. So HBO gave me more and more territories. In just a short time, my career trajectory has been steeper these last few years than all years combined since I started with HBO.

So no matter how long, keep dedicating time to discovering what you're passionate about.

Passion changes the game.

PURPOSE

If you are looking to achieve remarkable, fulfilling, and sustainable success, you must have both passion and purpose.

Passion is your feelings, your compelling emotions. Purpose is the *why* behind it all. It is the reason why you do what you do. Purpose sustains passion.

Passion can be wild and unbridled and have many different looks and feel. Again, you can be passionate about many things, like cooking, sports, movies. Purpose is usually singular and focused. Passion is for you; purpose is for others. How will you use your talents and gifts to serve the world?

One of the hottest topics in HR right now is employee engagement and retention. It's the second biggest talent-management challenge we're all facing. (Leadership development is #1.) Companies are trying to figure out the secret to becoming a "talent magnet" and then keeping employees engaged with a productive environment and meaningful work.

At the same time, employees are making the decision to "re-up" every day when it comes to motivation and productivity. Millennials in particular are looking for work that inspires passion and allows them to fulfill professional, personal, and social goals. Younger-generation employees are coming to work with a very different set of aspirations. We know that 70 percent of Millennials want to launch their own businesses at some point in their careers. Many of them don't mind working for smaller companies and want to work for organizations that are flexible and purpose-driven. So, any workplace that lags behind in inspiring passion and fulfilling purpose will suffer by losing key employees.

There is a landmark study by William Damon, a professor at Stanford, that took an in-depth look at the lives of young people. He studied two main groups:

- those who were confused, lost, lacked career motivation and were at serious risk for never finding a life pursuit
- those who were connected, highly engaged, and thriving (By the way, this was the smaller group.)

He found there was a key ingredient among youth who are thriving today and will go on to be successful adults: they have developed a sense of purpose in their lives even at an early age. It is the awareness of this purpose that provides them with motivation and direction.

Well heck, leaders need that too! Purpose provides motivation and direction.

Even if your purpose is not clear to you now, its okay. Go out and get involved with different things you care about. You don't need an all-consuming cause, but you do need something you care enough about to give up Facebook and Instagram for a little while.

My purpose? I believe the intention for my life is to touch, connect, engage, and inspire others to live the life they've imagined. It's the reason I wrote this book! I wanted to use my own life as a humble illustration on how you can move from where you are to where you want to be … and quickly. I wanted to help you carve a path forward to the best version of yourself and those around you. What good is it for you to grow and expand if it doesn't help those around you, too?

I am energized every time I share my purpose. The clarity feels good.

POWER

Author Marianne Williamson wrote one of my favorite passages:

> *Our deepest fear is not that we are inadequate.*
> *Our deepest fear is that we are powerful beyond measure …*

Power comes when you combine your passion and your purpose into a boundless, uncontainable force. The possibilities of that power are unstoppable. It's through your power you can make the biggest impact on the world, in your own life, and in the lives of those around you.

My passion is to bring people up and help them become their best selves—to see more in them than they see in themselves, and then help them to see it, harness it, and succeed. My purpose is to build highly functional and productive work teams. My power comes from leading teams in personal and professional growth to explode all previously held ideas of what was possible.

Embracing your power may mean that you launch yourself higher and higher on the corporate ladder … or it might mean you completely pivot and use your talents for something else, something that brings you an even greater sense of meaning in your life. Stories abound of people leaving the corporate world to become teachers or organic farmers or fundraisers for important causes. People take their skills and talents, developed in the corporate world, and find a way to combine them with their deep passion for helping worthy causes.

In 2015, I took an unconventional pivot at HBO that shocked many people; I left the glamorous, high-budget world of sales and marketing to take a leadership position in human resources. Honestly, people told me I was crazy, but I knew what I was doing. I was following my passion to help connect talents and gifts with opportunities to reveal diamonds hidden inside. My joy doesn't come from leading highly successful, highly functional teams. It comes from *creating* them.

PASSION + PURPOSE = POWER

PIT STOP!

Personal Ramp: You have your passion list and you know what you're passionate about, so what are you going to do about it? How can you embrace your passion, purpose, and power in your personal life?

____

____

____

____

____

Professional Ramp: What's your speed at work? Are you coasting, in the slow lane, or pedal to the metal? Is there something from your passion list that you can make a part of your resume?

____

____

____

____

____

TAKE TIME TO LISTEN AND LEARN

While juggling the demands of leadership, it's important to remember to pause long enough to listen to and learn from your team. During my first week as head of recruiting at HBO, I met my team of thirteen folks. There were a couple of managers, a few recruiters, some coordinators and assistants. On my very first day, I asked the team, "If you had one thing that could fundamentally change and improve how you work, how you handle business what would it be?"

They said, "We need iPads."

I was a little shocked. I said, "Wait a minute. You don't already have iPads?"

They shook their heads. "No. We only have BlackBerries."

How do you manage or see or at least get a full sense of a resume on a BlackBerry? Answer? You don't. At least not clearly. Which is why they were staying at the office late at night. Resume management was easier on the computer at their desks.

I said to myself, *If the biggest thing standing in a group of people's way to productivity and can be an easy morale boost is thirteen iPads, then let's make this simple thing happen.* By Friday, I had ordered thirteen iPads. In my previous department I'd seen my boss do the same and the positive impact on our business communications was remarkable. Remember, years earlier I had already put away fears of being fired and sometimes just moved on things that were just the right thing do and good for business.

On my first day in HR, I started having one-on-one's with the team, and by Wednesday one of the top recruiters turned in his resignation. He said he'd been sitting on it for the last two days. While he had already accepted another job outside the company and wanted to honor that agreement, he did hesitate because he wanted to see where my brand of leadership could take us. "Carla, you don't want us to just have job satisfaction," he said. "You're actually trying to create jobs we love."

I understood quickly how important this team was to the company. A talent acquisition department directly helps shape the DNA of the company. You especially don't want a recruiting team to be disgruntled or disengaged. You want them enthusiastic, invested, and thriving so they can throw open the gates to the people who shine—and close the gate on those who don't.

Here's what I learned: You have to keep your eye out for good people who may be in a bad situation. It shows they want to do more. They want to be more. And if you can turn things around and help them thrive, you can often find some of your best allies and future leaders.

You can learn a lot when you take time listen.

PIT STOP!

Personal Ramp: When was the last time you observed a leader doing something bold to serve their team? What about it was memorable?

____

____

____

____

Professional Ramp: How can you engage, listen, and learn from your team to power up and create jobs they love?

____

____

____

____

BRINGING PEOPLE UP

Some of the top issues, and therefore priorities, for business leaders are talent acquisition, engagement, and retention. We don't know, or forget, to prioritize leadership. The best way to address all three pain points at once is through *leadership transformation*—and I don't mean firing all the managers and bringing in new people. I mean transforming your own style of leadership so you create a place where fresh, new talent wants to work; where leaders say, "Yes," or "Let's explore further," when employees offer ideas; and where the best people stay and grow for long periods of time, adding the invaluable component of institutional knowledge, understanding the history and the inner workings of the company, as part of their skill set and worth.

If you are already years into your position at your company or organization, it can be hard to make a change—especially when your employees and team members already feel like they've got a handle on who you are and how you operate. But I guarantee if you start making changes, people *will* rise up to join you. It might not happen right away, but it will happen. (And, for those few people who resist, you can speak to them about alternative pathways to success for them, both inside and outside the organization … because the rest of your team is *moving on*.)

As you're planning, be bigger, be bolder! Think about who's on your team. How can you match talents that fit with your new agendas? Remember, if someone isn't clear about how they fit into the big picture, it's up to *you* to get them back in the loop. Employees must own their own development too, but you have to clear the way for them. If you give an instruction and the employee fails, roll it back and ask if you truly provided the information he or she needed to be successful. This may be hard to hear, but many of the problems on teams can be traced back to ineffective leadership. You're not there to beat people up. You're there to *bring* people up.

It's not enough to know where *you* are on the map. An enlightened leader makes sure everyone on his or her team is crystal clear about their own positions and how much progress they've made (or not made) on their path inside the overall mission of the team.

Remember, you want a floor full of showroom models—the fastest and brightest—a network of experts surrounding you and running at top speed with a clear understanding of the road ahead and what it will take to get to the next destination. Take time to help your team reassess, refuel, and re-up (shout out to *The Wire*) for the next big drive forward.

PIT STOP!

Personal Ramp: How can you connect family and friends to their passion or purpose?

____

____

____

Professional Ramp: What are some things I can do to fully prepare my team for the next stages and changes? How can I help them to become reflective thinkers, elevating their ability to assess what got them here and what they'll need to get them *there*?

____

____

____

LANE 8

"IF YOU WANT
TO GO FAST, GO
ALONE; IF YOU
WANT TO GO FAR,
GO WITH OTHERS."

—AFRICAN PROVERB

CHOOSE YOUR PASSENGERS

A few months before the tenth anniversary of my crash I was on a panel at a diverse teen girls conference held in Princeton and like many times before I was asked how did I go from a small town like Centerville to New York City? How did I become a vice president for a big company? My answer has and will always be the same: I made it on the wings, prayers and backs of those who came before me. I made it by standing on the shoulders of others, of those who saw greater in me, believed in me, lifted me up and gave me a chance to succeed. I was given special projects and opportunities by those above me to help me grow and level up. They saw my good work, my drive, my willingness to adapt and learn and space was made for my talent. You will not get places by yourself. You have to have others see you, believe in you, want to help you.

Certainly, I've always striven to deliver impeccable work, but advancement only comes from others' belief in you and advocation of you when you're not in the room. And that goes for any room: at work, at school, at home, at church, in life. Be the person who people want to be around and help you grow. If you are, one day you'll be in the position to pull someone else up and make space for his or her talent.

FUEL FOR THOUGHT

You *power up* by engaging your passion and purpose. Others help you *level up* by engaging your power.

A FOUNDATION OF SUPPORT

If you're going to carry the world, you'd better be planted on something solid. In the entire panoply of ideas and faith, there is nothing stronger than truth. Truth is a lightning rod that we shoot deep into the ground, anchoring us and holding us fast. Drive that lightning rod down far enough and you can hold up the entire world on your shoulders, like Atlas. What was Atlas standing on? Truth. From that base of truth, you can build out the rest of your life and everything you stand for—but you WILL need others to help you stand firm. You need to build a *network of support.* You need people who will cheer you on, hold you accountable, and even put up roadblocks from time to time for you to surmount. And you need people who aren't afraid to tell you the truth.

If you're really lucky (and believe me, "luck" in this respect just means you're diligent and paying attention), you'll find people who are on the same journey—or a similar journey—as your own. People with the same goals, who will keep you revved up, fueled, and engaged. Or who can even pick you up and carry you, from time to time.

IF YOU'RE REALLY LUCKY (AND BELIEVE ME, "LUCK" IN THIS RESPECT JUST MEANS YOU'RE DILIGENT AND PAYING ATTENTION), YOU'LL FIND PEOPLE WHO ARE ON THE SAME JOURNEY—OR A SIMILAR JOURNEY—AS YOUR OWN.

In this era, where time is at a premium and everyone is infinitely busy, we are losing an essential element of what makes us successful as humans——relationships. Real ones. Deep ones. Ones that last decades and beyond.

Professionally, we are working long, burdensome hours. In our personal lives, we're doing crazy amounts of over-parenting. In our private time, we're pouring our need to connect into social media at rates that mimic addiction. But step away from the panic, and you'll quickly see it's all false. The frenzied pace and panic of life is time consuming, overwhelming, and *false*.

Let's look at some basic engineering: A stool with three legs stands strong and steady, but put it on two legs and you've got a problem. Without perfect balance, the stool is destined to tip over and fall. It's even worse if you've only got one leg to stand on … one false move and you're sprawled on the floor. But three—that simple, magical number—*three* legs hold you strong and steady against the world, against gravity itself, which is a force so strong that nothing on earth can defy it for long.

With too many legs, the stool ceases to have a function. It certainly wouldn't support you any *better*, and all those legs would eventually start to get in the way.

Social media is much the same. There is a tipping point where support ceases to be *support* and is simply adornment … or clutter. Do you need five thousand likes and ten thousand followers at the start of your career? Does that really make a difference? Does it make a *positive* difference? I would argue that it doesn't. And, if you're working hard, who actually has the time or energy to maintain and upkeep a network of ten thousand people? Outsource the upkeep of your network to someone else, and they cease to be your connections at all, leaving you with a tangle of emotional and social clutter. Don't get me wrong, I think social media is a critical platform for networking success, personally and professionally. An inbox message from a friend you don't see much can come at just the right time. A large professional network can help you sell books! What I'm talking about is what you *really* need for the heart. What I'm talking about is truth. Your foundation of support.

To make it through emotionally, I believe you only need three essential people in your life—a "board of directors" to bounce things off of, to keep you on path, and to support you when you need some help and love. Three essential *anchor relationships* for three essential life spaces:

- **YOUR WORK:** You need someone in your professional life who can keep you honest and help provide clarity. Someone who cares about you genuinely and wants nothing in return but to see you win.
- **YOUR CIRCLE:** You need someone who is truly a good friend, someone who is honest with you about who you are and where you're going and isn't afraid to keep things real, even if he or she doesn't think you're going to like it. Someone who will do this out of love.
- **YOUR HOME:** You need someone who loves you for YOU, someone who just loves your face, your soul, your mind, your craziness. Someone who will still love you when your hair is falling out or when you can't even sit up straight. (A woman in a recent workshop I was facilitating added that if you're single, that person needs to be you! She's exactly right. It's called self-love.)

FUEL FOR THOUGHT

When it comes to mentors, go beyond the traditional champions, advocates, sponsors—those words seem less intimate, as if they describe someone who's only around for some of the good and very little of the bad. What I'm describing for these three are not those types of relationships. I'm talking about a *believer*, the one person who's not afraid of exploring the "good, bad, and ugly" with you. The person who's open to a tightly knit exchange of thoughts and ideas about you. Usually peers can't help you do this. Your believers, counselors, teachers, guides and gurus can. Write down one or two names right now. People who currently play a role in your life. You trust them, these are people who know you intimately as friends. When will you ask them to play these roles for you? You now have a definition of what these three people should be doing for you. "Truth-teller", sit down and have a truthful conversation with them.

The secret to getting these three people? Simple. *You need to be valued as one of these three key people in* their *lives.* (Hard to do if you're frittering away your few free moments clicking "like" or swiping left.) What are you adding to the world around you? What are you adding to the conversation at home or at work? What are you bringing to the table?

Think of all the beautiful things you can build with just three things. For example, if you have a vase and you put three blossoms in that vase, it is beautiful. Set it on a lovely table and it's elevated. Add a hundred other flowers and it's impressive, but those three blossoms were enough.

Working for a large company, I understand you have to have a powerfully extended network to do the really big business. But what are you going to build it on? Making sure your foundation is in place, no matter how simple or unassuming it appears to be, is never a waste. The strength of everything else you add will be underwritten by the strength and the worth of that foundation.

Build a strong base of three essential people, work authentically to build those relationships up, bring along the people who add value and can carry their own loads, and your success will be a byproduct of that work. It's genuine and authentic, delivering on the promise of the gifts you've been given to serve the world, in whatever way, shape, or form is true for you.

PIT STOP!

Personal Ramp: Who are your non-work anchor relationships? If they are not yet in place, how do you plan to cultivate them? Are you willing to be an anchor relationship in someone else's life? Are you already someone's anchor?

____

____

____

____

____

____

Professional Ramp: Who is your work anchor relationship? If you do not have one in place, how do you plan to cultivate it?

____

____

____

____

____

____

BEING A GO-TO LEADER

Even if you're at the beginning of your career, you can begin the process of selecting the passengers who will accompany you on your adventure by extending your networks and listening to other's ideas and opinions. Start to cultivate the vast network of committed individuals you will call on—and who will be there for you—as you travel forward into the wild. If you are already well on your way, take a serious look at who you are carrying along for the ride. Who are the passengers in your life? If you were in need, could they take the wheel? Or would everything crash without you? (And don't forget—you're also the passenger in other's lives … the faster you move together, the more closely aligned you'll need to be in your goals.)

LET'S FACE IT; YOU CAN CALL YOURSELF A LEADER BUT IF YOU LOOK BEHIND YOU AND NO ONE'S THERE, YOU'RE NOT A LEADER.

To be a successful leader, you need people behind you. Let's face it; you can call yourself a leader but if you look behind you and no one's there, you're not a leader. To keep people around, you need them by your side, not under your thumb. One of the best ways to do this is to help them continue to grow into well-rounded people who can stand on their own without leaning heavily on you. (They're in your car, remember? You need to make sure they all have their driver's licenses!) As you continue to benefit from your anchor of three quality relationships in all aspects of your life, you'll start to see ways to help your team members cultivate their own "trifectas of support."

As the leader, it's up to you to set the tone. If you see employees or team members floundering, isolated, or disconnected, you may need to take it upon yourself, as their leader, to help stabilize them by being a *go-to leader*. Get at least one of their support struts in place, then help them add or strengthen the second and third.

As you look at your team, think seriously: Are these the people you *meant* to pick up as your passengers? Are they destination-driven or are they dragging everything down? If some people are constantly dragging behind and/or sabotaging the progress of the group, take note. Then, take action. Either find a way to get them on board, or show them the exit. It will be better for you, for your team, *and* for them.

Many of us grew up with our parents or grandparents reminding us that "you are the company you keep" or "you can tell a lot about someone by who they choose as their friends." It's basically the social equivalent of "you are what you eat." There's wisdom in those old sayings. The people you choose to surround yourself with have an immediate and vital impact on your life. They are the people who open or close doors, who open or close minds, who generate or stop the flow of ideas, who give you a lift or drag you down.

PIT STOP!

Personal Ramp: What are new ways to cultivate stronger relationships in your life?

____

____

____

____

____

Professional Ramp: Knowing how important true human relationships are, what can you do to develop and strengthen them within your own team?

____

____

____

____

____

FIND YOUR "PERFECT AUDIENCE"

Writers sometimes talk about the "perfect reader"—someone who can read what you write and receive your words without a barrier, as if what they are reading simply unlocks or confirms ideas and beliefs already held within them. I believe the concept of the "perfect reader" extends into our lives in many ways: the best friends who feel more like siblings; special relationships between colleagues, partners, creative collaborators; the elusive "soul mate" sought after in romantic relationships. I also have found there is something akin to a "perfect audience"—an ideal group of people at the ideal moment who, collectively, reach up and enthusiastically accept what the speaker is trying to convey. I've seen it happen at church, at conferences, at political rallies and speeches, and at fundraisers with truly great causes.

I ALSO HAVE FOUND THERE IS SOMETHING AKIN TO A "PERFECT AUDIENCE"—AN IDEAL GROUP OF PEOPLE AT THE IDEAL MOMENT WHO, COLLECTIVELY, REACH UP AND ENTHUSIASTICALLY ACCEPT WHAT THE SPEAKER IS TRYING TO CONVEY.

Every leader has a perfect reader—a perfect audience—a group of people who can receive what you are trying to convey with no barriers, no judgment, no subterfuge, no secret desire to see you fail. People who immediately recognize you and the message you are delivering, making explanations unnecessary. People who want to reach toward your message and help you accomplish the great and grand tasks of your life, to bring your businesses and goals to the next level of achievement. People who will stand with you and follow your lead.

As leaders, we may hold the torch, but our audience and team members are the people whose voices swell behind us as we walk through the dark hours of the night, who urge us onward and carry us forward. It is important to find those people who can accept you without barriers, who can take the wholeness and fullness of who you are and receive it, lovingly, and connect completely with you and your mission. For me, this was the woman on my new team who immediately reached out to share thoughts and reactions after our first team huddle. She embraced me immediately and without judgment and question, because she saw the truthfulness of what I was saying and what I wanted for all of them. To this day, we talk about our first connection.

As we pivot from crash moments to leading through crash moments and beyond, it's worth taking a moment to look at the people you have gathered around you, because, as this chapter will show you, this is not a solo journey. You cannot do this alone. You must find your perfect audience and choose your passengers—deliberately decide who will be traveling with you—and who won't. It's time to look at the people you've gathered and make some choices. If you're not thrilled with the company you've assembled, then cull and cultivate that tribe—those perfect readers—and find people who can hear you and accept you without boundaries or borders.

"IF YOU WANT TO GO FAR, GO WITH OTHERS"

I lived the first half of my career and life, at home and at work, believing that no one knew better than me. If a problem needed solving or something needed to get moving, I was certain I might as well just pick it up and run with it, because there wasn't anyone better than me when it came to making things happen. Of course, that only got me so far. It's true that you can move very quickly when you're alone. You don't have to worry about extra weight, additional baggage, or other ideas, thoughts, or opinions. Your best idea is *the* best idea and you can run as fast as you can to make it happen.

Like the proverb says, *"If you want to go fast, go alone."* But as you gain experience and knowledge, you'll find that speed only gets you so far. That's when the second half of the proverb kicks in, *"But if you want to go far, go with others."* There is a critical moment when you realize that you don't have to be the smartest person in the room. To truly go the distance, you need other people to challenge you, to push you, to help you think deeper, see wider, go bigger, try harder. And they need you too.

In fact, without trustworthy companions on your journey, you fall into a risky place of believing that whatever you do, think, or say is the right path—possibly the *only* valid path. You're able to move quickly because you're not stopping to engage with the people who will test your philosophy or theory.

That doesn't mean everything needs a committee. There are times when you simply need to trust your own talents and gifts. I lived single most of my life, partially because I knew it was easier and quicker for me to pick up and do different things, change jobs, change my schedule, or change my city if I did it all alone.

There are periods where you *need* that alone time, that ability to trust your own intuition and instinct, your own knowledge, and your own experiences so you can grow your confidence. Always having check ins and making decisions by committee, can create some self-doubt—and yet input from others is good, too.

What I've come to learn is that I can take all the knowledge, experiences, and information that have been poured into me and mingle them with someone else's knowledge, experiences, and information. Now, suddenly, we can take it all to another level. We can go farther, into new territory. It's not about moving fast—although that can still happen—it's about going the distance. As long as your "far" includes helping others, you'll get there. Far is about maximizing the talents and gifts that you've been given in order to serve others. Your goal is to maximize the contribution of your gifts in a way that serves the world.

PIT STOP!

Personal Ramp: Describe what each of the anchor-relationships give you and how can you show them gratitude?

____

____

____

____

____

Professional Ramp: What are aspects of others at work that you admire and may want to emulate?

____

____

____

____

____

LANE 9

"WHAT YOU SEEK
IS SEEKING YOU."

—RUMI

GET BACK IN THE DRIVER'S SEAT

Crash moments are transformations in disguise: for you and everyone around you. The person who gets back in the driver's seat is not the same person who crashed. Your passengers aren't the same, either.

A few months before this writing, on a random evening, what started as a simple text conversation between my sisters and me led to a powerful moment of awareness that my transformation had touched them, too.

September 18, 2017 was the ten year anniversary of the crash, and I was just now really *hearing* what two of my three sisters think of me, the new me. At the same time, I was processing the great and positive impact *they* had on my development. None of us really knew the positive, transformative effects we had on one another until we connected the dots over a text chain one night.

SEPTEMBER 18, 2017 WAS THE TEN-YEAR ANNIVERSARY OF THE CRASH, AND I WAS JUST NOW REALLY *HEARING* WHAT TWO OF MY THREE SISTERS THINK OF ME, THE NEW ME.

That night, through our texts, we laughed and joked about what it was like growing up as an older (me), middle, and youngest sister. As adult women, I'm not sure we've ever spoke openly and truthfully about how we watched each other grow up, moved about in the world, and the lessons we taught each other. We unanimously agreed those sideline observations helped shaped each one of us today.

What did we uncover? We all agreed our eldest sister, Mimi, the most fiscally responsible one, taught us at an early age the value of money—how to save it, spend it, and enjoy it responsibly. I was ten when she started sending us $100 checks for Christmas to open up and build up our checking accounts. She was my first teacher of budget management, and now that fiscal responsibility has given me the ability to confidently manage and stand accountable for multi-million-dollar departmental corporate budgets.

My next younger sister has the sweetest way with people, due to her quiet and unassuming nature. Hobrina's ability to go with the flow and not cause too many ripples, taught me team play and temperance, both needed for successful leadership of any kind. For several years as a single parent, she always modeled resolve and fortitude.

And then there is Kindra, the youngest, "baby sis" (I still call her that). The most affectionate and most idyllic in her thinking and her view of the world, Kindra sees the highest of others and comes with soft, loving approaches. (I'm a bit more—well—clear and direct about how to get there). Kindra is one of the youngest and most decorated school principals in the Greater Atlanta area, and in large part because of her, I too see nothing less than one's maximum potential. I fight hard to ensure others can see, feel, and know their worth while also providing candid observations and areas for growth and development so they can win in every area.

What about me, the oldest? As far my contribution to the sibling collective, they told me it was my natural leadership ability, strong resolve and decision-making, and risk-taking that helped them learn to experiment and expand. They shared that seeing me reinvent my life, moving to different cities as a single woman, and traveling internationally, gave them permission to risk and try new things, too.

My crash moment made possible not only my transformation, but also this moment with my sisters. Your transformation can inspire others!

Crash moments are opportunities for transformation, to do things differently. These are the moments that take you way out of your comfort zone and give you a clearer perspective. These are the challenges that force you to create new pathways and find alternative solutions to put you on a higher level.

Someone once asked me if it was exhausting to carry this level of clarity and awareness day and night, and I answered emphatically, "YES!"

But what's the alternative? To live life unconsciously? To just go through the motions? To accept less than you're worth? To let a crash get the best of you and keep you down? No, thank you. I'll take my chances going with self-awareness, self-passion, and self-love in order to be strong enough to serve the world with intention.

With post-crash clarity and awareness connected to my 3P equation, I arrived at the calling of my life: to use it as a humble illustration to connect, engage, and inspire others to live the life they have imagined. You know from previous Lanes that I call this arrival *enlightened leadership*, and it was only achievable for me not only because of my one literal crash, but after experiencing multiple crash moments. Sound like a tough road? Well, I've found it's the only one worth traveling.

THE ROAD TO ENLIGHTENED LEADERSHIP

As a leader, having clarity and awareness about who you are and what you are here to do is essential for meaningful and impactful leadership. It makes you both humble and confident enough to release control and ownership of things. You release the need to prove how good you are and instead help others see how good THEY are.

Companies' biggest pain points today are around talent attraction, engagement, and retention. Could enlightened leadership help with that? You bet it could.

I believe when leaders change, teams change. When teams change, businesses change.

Junior (Taking)

Let's take it back to the beginning of my leadership road. As a new manager, I was all about *taking*. Asking others to "pick their brain" for clues and insights to success. Seeking others for connections and links into their networks to serve me. Jockeying for and taking positions to ensure I was seen and heard. I was concerned with making sure people knew how good I was. I was a perfectionist and often drove team members crazy with strong oversight of their work. I left little room for others to grow and showcase their skills.

While "taking" may sound bad, you should know it is not bad at all especially during this career phase. It is simply a necessary part of growth and development. In all actuality, when a leader is new he or she should ask a lot of questions, should seek out what worked well for those who succeeded, should ask for network connections, should ask others about their blind spots and pitfalls. New leaders who are serious about growing their careers should also certainly join industry organizations and become active in them.

The number-one organization that effectively changed the trajectory of my career is called NAMIC (National Association for Minorities in Cable, later changed to Multi-Ethnicity in Communications). I became a member the year I started in the industry in Atlanta, in 1995. I received Chapter Member of the Year award in 1996. When

I tell you I went in, I went all the way in. I recognized the importance this organization could have on my career and I believed in its mission to "be the premier media industry organization to educate and advocate for diversity in communications."

In fact, NAMIC made me a VP long before HBO did. After many years in NAMIC, and just a few short months of active service in Chicago, I became VP of the Chicago Chapter and subsequently President of the chapter. It was here where I learned and practiced sales pitching, budget management, negotiation, organizational governance, fundraising, and much more importantly, inspirational leadership. I learned in NAMIC how to engage and inspire others to achieve a common goal.

FUEL FOR THOUGHT

When you're a Junior leader or simply junior in your career, take all the training you can get. Take control of your learning and development. Take charge by volunteering and becoming active in your industry. Take from participation in an industry organization, church committee board, or sorority chapter to learn as much leadership as you can. Take the membership-chair role or fundraising role and get out front. Where else will you learn budget management, leadership, and governance in your junior years? It's time to take as much as you can from these experiences. Taking is a natural part of growth and development. If you don't want to start as a taker, you're looking at it the wrong way. I expect young people and recent college grads to take whatever they can from me—to ask me for coffee, to pick my brain, then take away the cards, contacts, and connections.

As a new leader, and as you become leadership-ready, it is easy to put only yourself first. To show and prove to the world how good you are is usually at the top of your list. And that's okay. Just know, ultimately, real winning is not in serving yourself but in using your talents and gifts in ways to serve others. I encourage you to connect your moves and motives to something greater than yourself. Say to yourself, "I'm learning this for me—and to help others someday."

Eventually, you reach a point after you've accumulated enough talent and experience, when you begin to realize you can accomplish more by sharing than taking. It even helps when you're staring failure or an uncertain future in the face and wondering: "there's got to be more to life than this!"

EVENTUALLY, YOU REACH A POINT AFTER YOU'VE ACCUMULATED ENOUGH TALENT AND EXPERIENCE, WHEN YOU BEGIN TO REALIZE YOU CAN ACCOMPLISH MORE BY SHARING THAN TAKING.

Mid-level (Sharing)

After some time, I found I was running toward a goal my soul didn't even really connect to. I didn't know who I was and years later couldn't believe who I had become. I forgot to lean on my faith, my upbringing, my mother's teachings. I needed to plug back into my Higher Power. I needed to grow my soul.

If it wasn't for the crash, I may have never achieved the clarity to transform.

After the crash, things started to get clearer about who I was, what I wanted, and what I was here to do. I asked myself, "what is my purpose." I was so green I didn't even know the power of the question. I did have enough clarity to know I was given a second chance and had to make good on it. As I got clearer and began to transform personally (not just physically but mentally, emotionally, spiritually) I noticed the positive impact it had on my leadership at work. I began to lead from a place of peace and authenticity, no longer feeling a need to compete and prove.

I wasn't really aware of something like enlightened leadership until a few days after the crash when I was trying to get back to work in bandages and my supervisor told me: "Carla don't go into the office still bruised and bandaged up. You will make others think they will have to do the same."

I have never forgotten those words and use them today in many situations as a metaphor. She was right. Even if I had a certain level of personal commitment to work for myself, the way my team may see and perceive me supersedes that.

She continued, "You don't have to prove you belong in this role. What you've already done got you here. You just need to focus on healing." After we hung up, I broke down in tears on the stairs in my home because my soul understood every word.

"I no longer need to prove myself because I'm already here" became a mantra. I began to carry a humble confidence in knowing who I am and what I am here for.

"I'm already here" meant not just "here" at the "mid-level", but here in the present, being engaged and alive. "Here" isn't just a thing, a title, or a level. Being here is being present, appreciating contributions being made and those of others. Clarity. Presence. It's a transition from proving to improving.

I've always known I had a passion for teaching and helping others succeed. I started sharing what I was learning about business and personal growth more freely with my team, and even outsiders. At this point, my team began to grow and expand. The members were happier and getting promoted quicker than other teams. To make a long story short, in just a short time, my career trajectory became steeper after my crash moment than in all the years since I started with HBO in 1997.

It is clarity and awareness that will get you through many crash moments. If you're clear and aware, crashes can transform you into an enlightened leader. Notice I say, "crashes." Plural. Because rarely will there be just the one.

IF YOU'RE CLEAR AND AWARE, CRASHES CAN TRANSFORM YOU INTO AN ENLIGHTENED LEADER. NOTICE I SAY, "CRASHES." PLURAL. RARELY WILL THERE BE JUST THE ONE.

I've learned the beauty of "crash moments" *is that you are building a muscle you can rely on for future situations that could take you down.* And rather than take you down, you learn how to use a crash to fuel your life and not fall.

After awhile, when yet another crash moment hits, your ability and likelihood to "walk away" is increased. When you practice devastation enough times, it no longer feels as catastrophic as the first.

FUEL FOR THOUGHT

When you're deep in a crash moment, be mindful of your self-talk. Stay away from dramatic, catastrophic language like "my life is over", "I'll never be the same", "My heart has been ripped out of me", etc.

No matter the trauma, remember, there's a part of you, that remains intact, indestructible, immaculate. This is called your *True Self* (more about this in Lane 10), your core, where your power resides. We just have to remind ourselves to move away from disastrous thinking. Do that, and your self-talk becomes your transformation. "I'm never gonna make it." becomes "I will make it through this."—which turns into you making it through and even winning.

So how do you keep a crash moment from being so devastating?

Three quick ways to turn a crash moment into a speed bump:

1. **Shift your self-talk.** Words create thoughts. Thoughts become life.

2. **Keep moving.** There's a notion that the devil can't catch you if you keep moving. So stay active. Devastation can't take root if you keep moving forward.

3. **Visualize where you want to be.** See yourself on the other side as who you want to be, and hold that image. Keep that image and let it take shape in your life.

Your life is not over. And no, it will not be the same. Because you'll be better.

It took surviving the crash for me to grow from Junior to Mid-level, from taking to sharing. And while you may not like it, the only way to move from leadership level to leadership level is by continuing to flex your "crash muscles"—by continuing to go through crash moments, or at least tough ones.

First, you'll need to tend to the basics just to maintain: stay hydrated, eat something, get some sleep. Then you'll be able to progress to higher levels of consciousness and awareness. Finally, you can do the one thing that can lift you out of a crash moment quickest *and* lead to the highest level of enlightened leadership: the executive giving level—you can start sharing what you learned from your crash.

FINALLY, YOU CAN DO THE ONE THING THAT CAN LIFT YOU OUT OF A CRASH MOMENT QUICKEST *AND* LEAD TO THE HIGHEST LEVEL OF ENLIGHTENED LEADERSHIP: THE EXECUTIVE GIVING LEVEL—YOU CAN START SHARING WHAT YOU LEARNED FROM YOUR CRASH.

I personally started sharing my thoughts and feelings. Just as I share the story of my crash with you in this book and with audiences on stage, I reached out to close friends and told my stories. I felt deeply, and I emoted without guilt. I've learned if you hold bad things in they are sure to manifest in other ways later—such as overeating, overspending, screaming at family, or having a short temper. It's simple. Secrets destroy the soul; share them to heal and grow.

Just know this period of your leadership is about getting humbly comfortable about your own talents and gifts and sharing those with others who are on their way. I believe the best leaders are looking for the *next* ones. Don't be afraid to share what you know. As I've said before, start hiring people smarter than you, delegate your desk to rising stars, share the spotlight so you can move on to higher levels of leadership.

Executive (Giving)

I now know and believe wholeheartedly that the effectiveness of your leadership is directly tied to your level of self-enlightenment and personal mastery. Having command of personal power supports risk taking and other next-level behaviors.

> Your executive-level transformation comes in the form of *giving*. These **five beliefs** will help you *give to transform* and become an enlightened leader:
>
> - Keep constant connection with who you are and what you're in it for.
> - Choices shape destiny.
> - Enlightenment is irreversible.
> - Stay in the wonder of your own uniqueness.
> - Plug in to your Higher-Power source.

Self-awareness is the conscious knowledge of your own feelings, motives, and desires. If you understand your purpose and what you're here to do, then, I repeat, there is no longer a need to compete and prove anything to others. It is your purpose that provides motivation and direction. In fact, you may find that self-awareness may cause you to want to give more of who you are.

My desire for giving and helping others to succeed has reached new heights. Currently, my new phrase is "I want to give myself away." Which means give more to others. I want to give what people need and want, and in doing so, I become more fulfilled and freed. There's no longer much worry on what happens next. I'm no longer afraid of being fired or called on the carpet; I just do what's right.

This release of control and authentic personal freedom comes from knowing and practicing certain beliefs each and every day.

First and foremost, you must keep the engine running. You have to keep constant connection to who you are and what you're in it for. You may remember the first lane of this book was all about knowing who you are. When you live with this type of certainty, no one outside of yourself can tell you who you are. Many people spend a lot of time telling others who they think they are, and those who are unclear simply accept it and go along with other people's program. Not me. Not anymore.

Certainly, there is room for feedback and performance critique—because no one is perfect. Of course, at this stage of my life and career, I've learned how to hear and receive feedback—but I decide what I apply. I consider the source, then decide if I want to shift or not, all the while being willing to accept the consequences if I don't.

Next, cement in your mind that choices shape destiny. Everything swirling about you right now good bad or ugly is due to your choices. Not anyone else's. Yours.

Enlightenment is irreversible. You can't unring a bell. You can't unlearn something you've learned. Learning is cumulative, and you get smarter each day. So, if you revert to old ways, please understand it's a conscious choice you are making. As many of our grandmothers used to say, "when you know better, you should do better."

Next, stay in the wonder of your own uniqueness. You must learn to root for yourself, to vote for yourself, to choose *you*. When you are able to keep yourself encouraged then you are free to encourage others without a second thought. Have you noticed the first people to give compliments seem to be comfortable with themselves? Cheer for yourself so you can freely cheer for others.

One huge aspect of a personal transformation is to plug into a Higher Power source. I am not one bit confused that how I got here today is not by my own doing. If left to my own devices, I would still be morbidly obese, unhappy, and lost. But I wanted more for my life, sought more, and knew it would come from outside of myself. One of my favorite quotes is "what you seek is seeking you." I found that reactivating my faith would fuel me to next levels and beyond. I had to get out of my own head and my own way to let my purpose come through.

When I took all these steps, my personal transformation was on and unstoppable—and so was my career. If you practice those five beliefs, you will be living and giving at the executive level of enlightened leadership. You will have transformed yourself and are now capable of helping to transform others into enlightened leaders.

Personal transformation *is* leadership transformation.

Junior—Taking

Mid-level—Giving

Executive—Sharing

FUEL FOR THOUGHT

When you release the need to prove how good you are and instead help others see how good *THEY* are, it's called enlightened leadership.

Here's what it looks like. It's being transparent and sharing larger business issues with your team and asking them to help solve problems with you. It's agreeing to a plan together, giving them necessary resources and then getting out of the way. It's allowing them to deliver on the promise of their own talents and gifts. There's no need for micromanaging when there's a shared understanding of where we are as a team and where we want to go. You—the enlightened leader—are giving them the space and the spotlight.

LANE 10

"YOU DESERVE TO LIVE A LIFE YOU ARE EXCITED ABOUT. TAKE CHARGE AND DON'T LET OTHERS MAKE YOU FORGET THAT."

—UNKNOWN

TAKE THE WHEEL

Today as a growth coach, transformation speaker, and leadership author, the connective tissue in all my leadership work is centered around my personal enlightenment and how to use that to pull out an individual's clarity and awareness about his or her own purpose—and then empower that person to live it.

Whether I'm speaking to hundreds of executives at a leadership conference or on a panel, connecting with readers on social media, hosting breakout sessions, or coaching in my one-on-one executive sessions, we unpack *you* before even addressing team issues. No matter your level, we begin and end with you.

GROWTH COACH

At a professional coaching certification program in 2016, I arrived at the first session with a sense of purpose and comfortable knowledge about myself and what I was there for. I was already eight years into *the new me*. I had been coaching without even knowing it. For years I had been helping myself and others move past the road blocks in their lives in order to achieve a better and more fulfilled way of living. I enrolled in the coaching certification program to learn about and implement the formal structure of coaching. I wanted to professionalize and build upon what I was already doing. I actually thought I would simply take notes for nine months and build my executive-coaching and training business, for others and not necessarily for myself. Even during our opening introductions, I said to the group I had already "done my work" and was here to learn how to provide formality and framework to my then informal and random coaching.

Never, and I mean never, had I been so wrong. I thought going from three hundred pounds to triathlete was the work. The affirmations, the journaling, the tears, the growth and the size 8 dress were all done. Surely after years of doing my work I was ready for the next level. In fact, it was during the very first class when I realized "my work" had just scratched the surface in order to complete a course like this. Everything I had done before the class was really just practice!

I realized (very quickly) this course wasn't for others as much as it was for me. The Coaching For Transformation Program (CFT) offered through the New York Open Center isn't just for aspiring coaches. It's for people who want to live their own lives on a higher plane, a more connected and aligned level for *themselves* and not to just to start a coaching business.

So many times this program knocked me off my feet, and many days I remained dazed.

I didn't know this level of self-awareness existed and that I would be called on it. Not only do you have to practice coaching others for hundreds of hours to become certified, you have to be coached yourself.

It was during these coaching sessions with other students and a certified professional coach when it really began to crystallize and take root in my soul and spirit who I really was. One of the most impactful days of my training came on day one.

The CFT program is a blend of classroom work, weekly teleclasses, and hours and hours of practicals. On my first teleclass call, the instructor laid the foundation for what this type of coaching is all about. And what he said immediately took me to another level. In essence, he said, "the true goal of coaching is to help others (and ourselves) find connection and alignment with themselves (ourselves.) And the Self, with a capital "S", is the very core of who you are. He said no matter the hurt, no matter the harm, or even with the most traumatic experiences, you cannot damage the True Self, the core. Even with all the hurt, there remains an intact, immaculate, indestructible part of you.

YOU CANNOT DAMAGE THE TRUE SELF, THE CORE. EVEN WITH ALL THE HURT, THERE REMAINS AN INTACT, IMMACULATE, INDESTRUCTIBLE PART OF YOU.

And it's in THAT part of you where your aliveness is, also your creativity, your imagination, your Higher Power, YOUR power. This is the Self you're born with. Everyone has it.

I learned, in that moment, that my Self is what I finally plugged into for my breakthrough. It's what you tap into to drop 100 pounds in a year and go from 300 pounds to triathlete. It's what you tap into to save marriages; it's the source from which you rekindle broken friendships; it's the Higher Power source you use to reconnect a family, even in the face of dysfunction.

I believe we already possess the power to change our very own lives.

In CFT, we believe coaches don't have the answers, we believe the person being coached already does. We just ask empowering questions to get you to clarity and awareness. One night, I was coaching a woman (via phone) who was in a new marriage and had a young child. She spoke of communication challenges with her husband and hurt and trauma in her childhood. But I saw very quickly she was very strong and opinionated. By the end of our forty-five-minute call she said she has never felt this grounded, this confident. Good coaching can be impactful very quickly. Hurt and disappointment don't have to be a burden, and don't have to take a whole lot of time to shift. A moment of enlightenment, a bit of clarity, a pivot can happen in a snap. It happened to her. It happened to me.

Within one of my own hour-long coaching sessions, my coach, Sharon, helped me see that the source of my decision making was still coming from a little girl and not the accomplished adult. I had to stare that thing down and learn to stay cognizant each day of who is in the driver's seat.

Since completing the course and graduating as a Certified Professional Coach, I've conducted more than 400 coaching sessions and have hundreds of emails, letters, notes, and cards from people who have said I've helped them. I weep in gratitude and joy each time I receive one. These words of affirmation make me feel I am certainly doing what I was meant to do.

Also in 2016, I purchased a business and sales coaching franchise called The Growth Coach. Entrepreneur Magazine ranked it as the fastest growing #1 business coaching franchise in the country. I often tell people I didn't find The Growth Coach, it found me. The Growth Coach is a unique coaching business that leverages the power of group coaching of entrepreneuers, small-business owners, and executives looking to create life and business breakthroughs. The curriculum is a patented process, simply and uniquely designed to help leaders work less, earn more, and get their lives back. The foundational principle this franchise is built on what I believe: You already possess the power to change your very own life. In other words, you already have the answers; sometimes you just need help asking the right questions.

In the process of becoming a certified professional coach and a Growth Coach franchisee owner all the ideas and theories I had about leadership and delegation became concrete. I learned to refine and truly articulate a business leader's purpose and help individuals and teams to find their own. With this vocabulary, I'm happy to share this learning with others, connecting with people more deeply and directly and with a healthy sense of vulnerability. I certainly have no hesitation sharing wins and losses, peaks and valleys in my career and in life.

LEADERSHIP AUTHOR

With this new *formalized* framework for life and business success, along with an elevated vocabulary, I give my stories voice through speaking and writing. Writing means a lot to me because I am able to express without compromise or debate. I am free to share what's on my mind and give what's in my heart to help others. This is my way to humbly serve the world. Give everything I know away to others.

A few months before I started writing this book, I was sitting in the backseat of my sister's car as she was taking my niece and nephew to soccer practice. (I was in the back to separate the two from each other during one of their big sis/little brother moments.) My sister, then a middle-school principal—and who has a big, creative, wildly imaginative mind like I do—quickly jumped in when I said I wanted to write a book about personal transformation and its impact on life and career. Neither of us had any idea where to start, but within just a few minutes I had grabbed my notebook and we began to outline my chapters (later I called "lanes"), break them down into topics, and even played around with book titles. I named this book and even the subtitles in the car that day.

Over the course of the next few months, thoughts on what I would write about began to flood my mind, and I had to type it out. I was being asked to speak more and more, and the stories that would come out in those moments also became text for this book.

I began to meet a lot of people who wanted to hear more about my transformation, and while I couldn't connect with everyone by phone, I had detailed afterhours and weekend e-mail conversations, which are now part of this book. I didn't know then the impact and power of words on paper. You can always reference or go back to printed words and phrases that moved you; and be energized and inspired all over again. The written word is an important part of my coaching. My clients say they enjoy re-reading both the supportive and fierce parts of my email notes.

It was Momma who gave us the love of books and reading. She has always been an avid, voracious reader. Even now (at this writing) she keeps at least five books on her nightstand and reads a minimum of two of them a week. The big, thick autobiographies of famous or infamous people are her favorite. I wonder what she is thinking as she reads about herself in this one! She will probably smile as she falls asleep with her glasses on like she always does.

I'm glad I've moved beyond being afraid of opening up to the world this way—especially if it means illuminating the conversation of truth-telling and enlightened leadership. I am eager to share my thoughts, pitfalls, blindspots, and learning experiences on my budding blogs, websites, future books and becoming a future contributing editor to Forbes.com. Contribution is one of my core values and living and working this way are what dreams are made of.

TRANSFORMATION SPEAKER

I started out as a sales trainer with HBO more than twenty years ago and, according to my math, since graduating from CFT, and in addition to all my work with HBO and industry organizations delivering keynotes, presentations, breakout sessions and seated on many panels, I can humbly say I have addressed over 10,000 people.

When I first started speaking, I accepted all offers—panels, breakout facilitation, speed coaching, mentoring, college events, new hire classes, young entrepreneurs' groups, teachers' associations, you name it. I accepted everything in any industry. Before long, I had racked up thousands of hours of speaking. I was greatly humbled and bowled over each time people would line up to meet me after speaking, and I hoped I had given everyone some of what they needed. I am still in contact with many people I've met over the years.

But nothing compares to my first official *big* speaking gig. I was the closing keynote speaker for an organization called Network of Executive Women (NEW). There were over 2,000 women *and* men in the Dallas Convention Center. They had just completed three days of workshops, seminars, and panel discussions on personal power—my jam.

I had never spoken in a room so big, with so many beautifully set tables, and so many monitors hanging from the ceiling. Soon after my arrival for a quick run through, the entire conference hall was filled. Next thing I know I was being introduced. I jumped on stage to the song "LET'S GO" by Calvin Harris and Neyo, and the crowd was on its feet—at 10 o'clock am!

We took a ride that morning—spotlight on my face, a country girl from Tennessee, and me giving all of my heart to the people. We talked about how to use personal power to transform your leadership and your life. I left everything on that stage that wonderful morning. I was again honored, humbled, and affirmed by the standing ovation forty-five minutes later.

Afterwards, the president made some final remarks and quickly adjourned the conference. I thought it was over. But it wasn't.

What happened next was a vision I will never forget: A line started forming to meet me, and it stretched to the back of the conference center! People were standing patiently, holding their phones, ready for pictures and one-on-one time with me. People shared whatever parts of my story was theirs.

PEOPLE SHARED WHATEVER PARTS OF MY STORY WAS THEIRS.

One woman said she believed her attendance at the whole conference was just to hear me. She cried and I cried, from the first one to the last. It took almost another hour and a half to greet each one individually. Each of those people that day touched me as well.

I later found out that audience members were live-tweeting my quotes, and I was trending in the conference app—not just that day but throughout the weekend! All weekend even when we were all back home, people kept posting about what I shared. I read quotes about how my speaking had inspired them to move, to shift.

This is the calling on my life: to touch, connect, engage and inspire others to live the life they've imagined.

The Real Work
by Wendell Berry

It may be that when we no longer know what to do
we have come to our real work,

and that when we no longer know which way to go
we have come to our real journey.

The mind that is not baffled is not employed.

The impeded stream is the one that sings.

FULL SPEED WITH THE TOP DOWN

As you get back in the driver's seat and take control of the wheel, I want to share with you the stories of others who've traveled the same road I have. These are people I've met through coaching, speaking, and writing. They're driving the lanes, on the road to learning the skills, experience—and clarity around who they are; they're asking themselves the right questions; they're gaining a good sense of their own worth.

Just as people at my speaking engagements share with me the parts of my story that are theirs, I want to share with you now the stories of others that may be yours, too:

> "Carla, I finally know my make and model, which allowed me, one day a few months ago, to stop letting my nerves get the best of me and give a presentation to my team. After I gave one, I gave a few more. Today my boss asked me to present to senior leader-

ship of the company. For the longest time, that request would have terrified me. Now, I'm excited." **—Karen D.**

"I spent ten years working, mostly, two mindless jobs. One was as a theater usher. When I thought about what I'd want to do tomorrow if today I barely survived a car crash, my first thought was of the theater. I'd been working as an usher in the dark so long that I'd forgotten that the spotlight was an option. It's there for me, too, isn't it? Now I don't just work in the aisles. I stare at my destination and work toward it." **—Sarah K.**

"As a young African-American professional, it was truly inspiring to see someone be their complete self in the work place, and it gave me the confidence to do the same. I know that privilege comes with hard work and time; there's no denying that. However, the conversation we had yesterday inspired me to earn that right, to motivate my peers to do the same, and above all do things consistently to challenge myself to achieve. The more I learn, the more I can teach, and one day I hope to motivate and inspire young people the way you did for me." **—Tyler J.**

"You helped me see how I've been dominating the spotlight at the expense of my team members, when in fact I should be making them shine. They have the talents and skills, it's up to me to help them share those. After all, as a leader, that's what my role really is, isn't it?" **—Samantha V.**

"I was stagnant in my career and other areas of my life. I was clear about what I loved, filmmaking, but didn't know how to change my situation or even move in that direction. I also had low self-esteem and didn't like the way I showed up. Carla helped me see my own worth, one piece of myself at a time. Once I got stronger, I made bolder and bolder decisions; the biggest one was when I decided to move to LA. Carla shared in my dreams and helped me step into them!" **—Chris S.**

"Carla's Transformation Workshop helped me realize there could be many pathways to my intended destination. All this time I was thinking I was in the wrong job at the wrong company. Instead, I'm where I'm supposed to be. I just have to see where this path connects with my next step. With this new lens, I've been making new connections ever since." **—Janice P.**

"I was unhappy with my finance job for a long time because I wanted to do something more creative. I wanted to make and sell jewelry. After a few coaching sessions, Carla helped me see my purpose and understand my power. My confidence grew, and ideas flowed. Last year, my sister and I opened our online jewelry business and it's wildly successful." **—Tiffany J.**

"During one of my sessions with Carla, I realized the people I kept around me are a reflection of me and how I view myself. The more I learned to trust and value myself, the more my friend circle started to change. I now feel more comfortable and supported by those who I call friends." **—Michelle S.**

"Driving—the feeling of freedom as you head out on the highway with no one's agenda but your own—is one of the most exhilarating feelings in the entire world. Driving your life according to your own purposeful plan and watching the road expand before you is fantastic. My mom and my wife's mom both passed away in the span of a month. For the longest time, we thought grief was driving our life. Now I know it's still us. We're back in the driver's seat." **—Samir M.**

As you take the wheel, here is a little summing-up for you:

Know your make and model. Stay vigilant on your destination. Read the signs and watch for signals. Quickly assess situations or people who are getting you closer or taking you farther from your goals.

Review crash moments, because they will happen. Explore the clarity they reveal about you.

Follow your roadmap … and your heart.

Most importantly, get back in the driver's seat, take the wheel and take control.

Drive full speed towards your chosen destination …
with the top down!

—Carla M.

4 PIT STOP BOOKS THAT HELPED ME TRANSFORM

Self Matters
by Dr. Phil

You Can Heal Your Life
by Louise Hay

The Four Agreements
by Don Miguel Ruiz

How The World Sees You
by Sally Hogshead

CONNECT WITH CARLA

In addition to her fun and fulfilling day job at HBO, Carla is an aspiring blogger, transformation speaker, and certified professional coach.

Carla is an active public speaker, delivering conference keynotes and facilitating workshops on a variety of subjects including leadership, personal power, and career design. Carla also is a popular panelist at leadership summits, industry events, and career fairs.

Signature Keynotes

"CRASHING Your Way To Success"
"Using Personal Power to Transform Your Leadership"
"Passion + Purpose = Power"
"Crash. Breathe. Drive. "

Popular Breakout Sessions ("Crash Courses")

- CRASH! Transformation Workshop
- Leadership Lessons from Game of Thrones
- Personal Branding
- Career Navigation

Also available for moderating panels, event hosting, corporate lunch and learn events

Book Carla for your next event!

cmoorespeaks@carlamoore.com • 917-951-2020

Follow me on:    

Join Carla's Community at carlamoore.com to receive a monthly newsletter for more conversations and inspirations, leadership tools, and speaking appearances!